One Time Around

Around

One Big Loop around
a Great Big Country

by Paul Clipper

To OHo
PVR 2017
[signature]

Prologue

In the summer of 2010, I decided to take a long ride on my motorcycle. The thinking behind it, and the reasons for such a journey are all covered in the story that follows, so there's no real need to go deep into all the "whys" right now. The bottom line is, for the first time in my adult life, I had time on my hands. And I literally had nothing else to do.

Oh, it would have been simple to stay home in southern New Hampshire and paint the house, cut the grass, fix all the things that had been neglected around the homestead in the past three years. Or I could even have panicked and looked for a job, gotten right back into the money-making trap. No, that's what I would have done in the past. I considered all the options carefully and decided that I was going to occupy my time this particular summer spending money rather than worrying about making it.

Why not? Time was running out on this sort of thing. I was in my mid-fifties. I could look down at my hands and be amazed at how mangled and distorted all my fingers are, as they erode from inherited arthritis. Already there were a number of things I couldn't do anymore—or maybe I could still do, but suffered a lot of pain while doing it. Like dirt bike riding. Playing a guitar. Hell, painting, working on a bike, or even typing. I was at a point they, in this new century, now call "middle age," as if we're all going to live to 100. That ain't gonna happen. How long would it be until my hands just didn't work any more, and I couldn't even ride a street bike?

Besides that, I had no wife, no steady girlfriend at home, nobody to answer to if I chose not to stay there. No kids needing college payments any more, not even a pet that depended on me to bring food home to him. In a word, I was just plain free; free to do whatever I wanted.

I had driven across the country a couple times in a car, and I found it interesting but maybe a little unsatisfying. There are people pleasures available in an automobile that are not to be slighted. You can crank the air conditioning up, turn on the music, sip champagne and eat a multi-course meal while roaring across Iowa; I've done it. I've felt the visceral joy of eating cole slaw with my fingers at 80 mph on the Jersey Turnpike, and it is a fine pleasure. But, I wanted to do it right this time. I wanted to cross the country and I wanted to feel it for a change.

To that end, I worked on the bike enough to ensure it was comfortable to ride, and made preparations to go. My plan was to make it up as I went along. I wasn't going to set any hard and fixed destinations, and I wasn't going to obsess over any particular roads or routes ahead of time. I was just going to go, and wander west until water stopped me, then I'd turn left. There would be no reservations, and hopefully no plans, but that didn't work out exactly right, and you'll read about all that later. The main point was that I was going to try to just follow my nose and make it up as I went along, and for the most part I think that's what I did.

My neighbor Bob, a good friend, took to likening my trip to Steinbeck's Travels With Charley after I told him about my intentions. That made me uncomfortable. Just because a person writes words down for a living, and has a yen to travel across the country for no particular reason, doesn't put him in the same game as one of the greatest American authors in history. I couldn't play on John Steinbeck's team on my best day, I don't even think I'm involved in the same sport. Whenever Bob talked about it—he called my trip *Travels With Gnarly*, which is a title I do really like—it just made me cringe.

But once I got out on the road, and had time to think about it, I came to the conclusion that Bob might be somewhat correct. Steinbeck is gone now, he can't present his side of the case. But what if—and he hinted at this in the above-mentioned book—what if he just wanted to get out, go for a long drive to clear his head; and, since his publisher would print anything he wrote down neatly, why not write a damn book and get his expenses back, at least?

If that was really the case, then you could make an argument that the only thing separating me and Steinbeck in this matter is the question of opportunity. He could publish a laundry list, if he liked (and I think his laundry lists were covered adequately after his death). I, on the other hand, have to resort to some sort of a back door, vanity publishing method to get my story out.

And that's why you're reading this.

What happened was, I kept a journal while I was out on the road. When I got back, just for the hell of it, I uploaded said journal to my Amazon Kindle, and one day while I was hanging out at my sister's house, I showed it to her. She started reading it, and got absorbed. After a while she said, "Hey, you know, this is really good. You should clean this up and publish it."

Coming from most any of my other friends, I don't think I would have paid much attention. But my sister, Robbie, is a tenured college professor with "Ph.D." after her name, and a creative writing teacher as well as published author of two books of fiction. She's also a helluva body surfer. She would be surprised to hear me say this, but she's one of the few people out there whose opinion I might respect.

So, what you're about to read is all her fault. I make no other excuse than that.

What follows is a travelogue, pretty much, with a little bit of rambling here and there. I don't know about you, but I'm a sucker for travelogues. Every time I see someone's motorcycle story in a magazine, I wind up reading it, and I've worked my way through almost all those 'round the world books that you see in the Aerostich catalog. I just find it fascinating what people are willing to go through, and what their problem solving process might be. If I didn't like to read that kind of thing, I doubt if I would have ever given Rob's idea a second thought.

But I did, and after fussing over it for a few months longer than I expected it to take, here's the finished product: a cleaned up, fleshed out and hopefully somewhat correctly edited story of what I did in the summer of 2010. I hope you enjoy it.

Paul Clipper
Richmond, NH 7/30/2011

One Time Around

One Big Loop around
a Great Big Country

7/15/10 Thursday

I was surprised that it took me all morning to finish packing the bike. There's only so much you can carry in two saddlebags and a topcase, and most of my "packing" consisted of taking things back out of the bags after deciding to leave them behind, and then putting other things in their place. Back and forth, in and out of the house as I danced this pointless dance, and all the while the mercury kept climbing on the thermometer. It was the middle of July. How much of this cold weather gear was I really going to need?

"Some of it..." was the answer. I had been on enough bike trips to know that no matter what, the weather was going to change. I also was experienced enough to know that yes, I probably was packing the wrong things, and I'm not going to find out what is needed and what is useless until I've been on the road for a week or two. Beyond having a good pair of jeans, a comfortable pair of shoes, and the right T-shirts in the bag, everything else was going to be shuffled around until I settled into a rhythm. That should be lesson one: most of what you're fretting about is pointless. You need extra clothes and raingear, and something warm. Throw them in the bags and get going.

Meanwhile, noon came and went, so I stopped for lunch, scraping together whatever was left in the house. It wasn't much. Peanut butter and crackers, at the most, which were going to get packed on the bike anyhow. Aside from them, the cupboard was bare.

I would have liked to say that this whole rigmarole was the final preparation after months of planning and research, but that wouldn't be true. The summer previous, I had started buying bikes that I thought might be suitable for a cross country trip, and just trying them on. I had reluctantly decided that I'd had enough of the business I owned, after 24 years, and thought that if everything worked out I could wind up with at least a small period of time where I could do whatever I wanted. And maybe I wanted to ride across the country. Even as I was finishing packing, I still wasn't really sure.

I bought a couple older BMWs—K75s--and wound up not liking either of them. One was a touring bike, with no breeze behind the huge fairing, the other was a sportbike with a back-breaking riding position. I sold the BMWs and considered a number of other machines, but friends in the business kept recommending the same bike: a Suzuki V-Strom; and preferably the 650 if I could get by with less horsepower. Honestly, I was really hesitant on the idea of buying a Suzuki. I had owned various Suzukis before and was never really impressed with them. But when everyone recommended the same bike, I eventually gave in and decided to try one.

I found one quickly enough, from a guy in Rhode Island selling it for his brother. The bike had 10,000 miles on it, not a speck of dirt nor a scratch anywhere, and as I looked it over the price kept coming down. I finally bought it at a true bargain price, and took it home in my van.

The V-Strom worked out really well. It was more or less comfortable, ran fairly well, and I knew I could iron out the few kinks I'd found. I rode it the rest of that fall then put it away when the snow started flying. In the spring of 2010, I started fiddling with it, making a myriad of minor adjustments that I'll talk about in passing as this story flows along. Basically I was happy with the bike in spite of my earlier prejudices, and knew it had great possibilities as a cross-country mount—even though it was only a little 650 twin. But I had ridden a friend's DL1000 V-Strom, and decided that just enough engine would be better than too much.

I'd been thinking seriously about hitting the road since late winter, when it became certain that I was going to have time on my hands. But as far as actually working on it, preparing it for a real trip—maybe I started on it a month earlier. All the work before that was centered around making the bike completely comfortable and rideable, and that had started the previous fall. I had actually spent weeks working on what handlebars to use, and whether to use risers and where to finally set the bar position. Then there was a cold-starting problem that was solved when I finally learned how to tune the V-Strom with an ohm meter, which was a unique experience for an old shade-tree mechanic.

Only in the last two days did the packing start, and eventually there was nothing left to pack or unpack. I locked the door to the house, hid the key and put on my helmet. At 1:20 p.m. I carefully eased a shaky leg over this unfamiliar bundle of bike and luggage, and thumbed the engine to life. The temperature was 90 degrees plus; it was my absolute least favorite kind of weather to be riding in. "Head north, as fast as possible..." I said to myself. Nudged it into gear, stalled the surprisingly heavy bike, re-started, rolled down the driveway, cruised the quarter-mile up to the center of town, hooked a left onto Route 32, and I was off. I was headed north, and glad to be done with all that pre-ride crap. It's like moving your house, but not taking anything with you. Within two miles I remembered a set of brake pads I'd left behind on the workbench, but decided to leave them there. My neighbor promised to mail me anything I'd accidentally left behind, and they would be the first thing on the list.

I stopped by my local hangout, Vintage Eddie's bike shop in Swanzey, for a bon voyage photo. Eddie said, "You know, you've got not much more than a thousand miles left on that rear tire." Aran, the mechanic, told me that our mutual friend Randy had just come back from Tennessee, and he had seen cords showing on his rear tire when he left Tennessee! "You might be able to make it to Denver..." They got me worrying about it, so I went an hour north and stopped at Mason Racing in Lebanon for a new rear tire. Luckily Clint had the right size tire, a Bridgestone Trailwing. While they were mounting it, I tried to cool off and have a look around.

Clint's shop is located in a small old mill building, just like a lot of the modern businesses in northern New England. They're all perched next to a stream or a river tributary, and Mason Racing is no different. A small stream rushes by behind the building, and I tried to make myself comfortable out there, trying to get used to the warm weather as well as looking to the water as an inspiration to cool off. It wasn't working very well, but the shop mechanic did a good job quickly, and I was back on the road in just under an hour.

Since it was late in the afternoon, I figured it would be best to make up some time and scoot to Burlington on Route 89. All I can say is, it was hot. Hot and humid. Felt like a hundred degrees on the road, not at all my kind of riding conditions. As a matter of fact, my inclination was to ride back to the ranch and put this whole thing off until the weather cooled down. But I didn't. How long would that take? It could have been one of those summers that just don't let off until October. At that point, I'd be starting too late. If I was going to take this trip it was time to get it started, I had already waited too long.

Why leave in July, if you hate hot weather? Well, it just worked out that way. The first major stop on this trip would be Colorado, and there's only a small window of time out of the year when Colorado is rideable, at least at the high altitudes, so that had to be considered. There was also a surfing trip planned—body surfing—for the Jersey shore in early July, with my girlfriend, my sister and my kids, and body surfing may just be the earliest passion in my life; born way back when I was a kid and my mother would take me and my sister to the beach. I wouldn't miss that for anything.

Also, I had legal issues, related to the sale of my business, to hold my attention until June first. Once June rolled around, and I was officially without a "visible means of support," I had no excuses left. I'd been telling people I would be retired 'til the money ran out, and at that point I'd revert to "unemployed." Whatever you call it, for the first time in my adult life, here in July of 2010, I literally had nothing to do. The best thing, then, was to take the "motorcycle trip I'd always dreamed of" and get it out of my system.

The funny thing was, I hadn't really dreamed about taking this trip. I'm sure I had mentioned once or twice that it would be interesting to ride a motorcycle across the country. I had done it in a car a couple of times, and that was, ummm...what? Impressive, maybe? It's a long drive. You can take a wandering route and see a lot of things. But looking back, it was restrictive, in its way, in a way that's only obvious to a motorcycle rider—or a bicyclist, a walker, whatever—like you're spending time in a cage all the way there. All of us two-wheeled aficionados know what it feels like to have the wind in your face, and I was curious. Every distance seems longer when you're out in the elements, and I wondered if this country would seem outrageously huge on a motorcycle; especially a fairly small motorcycle.

So my girlfriend said, "You should go. Now's the time to do that trip you've always talked about!"

I mused about it on the baking-hot ride to Burlington, on the first day of my big trip. I didn't really think I'd talked about it that much, but she would know. She is, by my best reckoning, always right.

My idea was to find a downtown hotel/motel/whatever in Burlington, get out onto the pedestrian part of the town and find a good spot on a sidewalk cafe to have a couple drinks and relax, get into the right frame of mind for the trip. I learned about a week into the ride to not have any expectations, but here on the first day I was setting myself up for disappointment. There were no downtown motels in Burlington, at least none I could find. I didn't want to park somewhere and hang out for a while, then get back on the bike in plus-90 degree weather and ride off looking for a place to sleep. I wanted to find a room, park the bike and be done with it. The whole day had been like riding straight into a blow drier, and I was thoroughly cooked.

I found a motel in South Burlington, the Anchorage Motel, with an Outback Steakhouse next door. Got a margarita as big as a stainless steel hospital bucket and a piece of red meat and I was finally comfortable. All I craved at that point was air conditioning and lack of burning sunlight; and though I remember little about that motel, I know it supplied shade.

I was hoping the next day would be a better day. Smaller road, slower speeds and possibly tree shade along the way. And, starting with an hour-long ferry ride across Lake Champlain ought to be fun. I thought that tomorrow would be the day the trip would really start.

The guy and the bike.

7/16/10 Friday

I woke up early, checked the ferry times again and realized I could catch the early ferry at 7:30. So I packed up all the stuff and zipped out of there, with just a motel donut and a single cup of coffee—after spilling the first one on the floor. I stopped at a traffic light at the bottom of Main Street, and watched the south end of a northbound girl dog-walker at a red light, thinking, "My, what an entertaining behind..." Right then Fido gave me a little bit of a treat by crossing around behind her and dragging her filmy nylon shorts way high with the leash, showing me just exactly how cheeky she really was. I had to laugh. Great way to start the day.

Burlington is a neat little city. It sits on the shores of Lake Champlain and right off the southern edge of Canada. Downtown is an appealing hodge-podge of low buildings and an easily navigable grid of comfortable streets. It's definitely a college town—four or five colleges make their home there—so consequently the populace appears young and active. The focal point of the town is a four-block pedestrian mall on Church Street, full of shops and sidewalk cafes, and it's an excellent place to sit and watch the population stroll by. Winters are so brutal in Burlington that on a warm summer day such as this absolutely no one remains inside, and the sidewalks were already filling with folks taking advantage of the warm weather. At a later point of the trip I know I would have been easily persuaded to lay back at a metal table on the Church Street Marketplace and linger over coffee and breakfast, or a beer or two later on in the day, and take in the scene. But on this morning, rolling down the hill on Main Street, heading for the ferry docks, reminded me just a little bit of San Francisco; and I was anxious to get this trip headed west.

I shared the ferry with a large group of road bicyclists out for a quick spin in New York. Like road bicyclists everywhere, they kept to themselves and eyed me with a little bit of discomfort. I find that road bikers, pedal bikers, hate everything else on the road--car, motorcycle or Amish buggy--and are basically miserable unless they're among their own. Little I cared. I've never been a big fan of anyone who thought they should own the road, bicyclist, motorhome driver, logging truck or moose. Instead of dwelling on it I concentrated on drinking coffee and examining the map for the right route to take through the Adirondacks.

Though Burlington is small, it's a busy, bustling little town. Port Kent, on the other side of the lake, is a tiny group of buildings huddled close to the rocky shore. Quiet and definitely rural. We docked with no issues and I followed Team Spandex off the boat.

My plan was to take a diagonal path through the Adirondack Forest, checking out Lake Placid and all those Olympics sites (1932 and 1980). The first stop was the toll road to the top of Whiteface

Mountain, 4865 feet, and the scene of the 1980 Olympics. From the bottom the ski runs look appallingly steep. Makes me think that one day I'd like to come try skiing it. The toll road runs to the top, where you have the choice of walking up to the summit via a gift store, apparently, or walk into a long tunnel and take an elevator 480-some feet to the top. Since the ride up on the bike already brought me into the clouds, and visibility was near zero, I opted for the elevator.

Once up at the top it was impossible to see anything. It seemed high, though. Back down to the bike and the rain was coming down.

Thundershowers had been forecast for the day, so it wasn't much of a surprise. What was a surprise was the intensity of the rain. I started out in the morning with Gore-Tex Aerostich gear, and I was glad to have it on. For a few short minutes, I thought that a cool rain would be a welcome relief. But, after the broiler of yesterday, the pounding rain and overall damp made the temperatures actually chilly.

I weathered the first shower okay, and every time I started thinking about stopping, the rain would stop so I'd roll on. I'd have just enough clear air to start drying out, and then here would come another shower. The third time this happened the rain just about pounded me off the bike, so I started looking in earnest for a place to stop for a while.

What you really want is a covered parking canopy outside of a neat local coffee shop. Next door to a bakery. I can tell you that that doesn't happen often. It never happened in the Adirondacks. Luckily though, when I was weariest and thinking I was going to drown from the pouring rain, I found a covered parking area at the Adirondack Museum outside of Blue Mountain Lake. Nice. I had a chance to shake out the gear and put on my vest for warmth, then get a cup of coffee in the museum gift shop. The coffee went well with the peanut butter and bread I'd been carrying in the top box.

Gore-Tex gear is a godsend in this kind of weather, but make no mistake, you still get wet. The Gore membrane—in the best of riding gear—keeps you dry on the inside, but the outer skin of the jackets and pants get soaking wet, of course. All this running water on your exterior is like a heat-sink, and over time it sucks so much heat out of you that there's no way to stay warm without outside help. For this, I had an Aerostich Kanetsu electric vest, and that's what I put on in the museum parking lot. It felt really ridiculous putting on an electric vest the day after 95 degree temperatures, but that fine plug-in garment would come in handy for the rest of the trip.

I also had one of those wet-vests on board; a kind of a quilted vest that soaks up water and holds it in. You wear it under your jacket in extreme heat and it'll knock your core temperature down to the point that the heat becomes bearable. I could have used it and enjoyed it the day before, but the thought of putting a slimy wet thing on over dry clothes (like a T-shirt) didn't appeal to me at the time. Dumb. Something I'm going to have to get over one of these days.

The only other gear issue was my choice of boots. I started the ride with a pair of Sidi vented road boots made out of Lorica, a fancy name for artificial leather. The vented feature was something new to me, and I was madly in love with them during the shake-down rides in previous weeks. I still liked them fine, but the vents also let water in quickly—and completely. My feet were soaked five minutes into the first rain storm. It'd be nice if they could make boots with closable, waterproof vents.

I left the museum parking lot when the rain slowed, electric vest turned to "high" on the 16th of July. After a while the rain stopped and I got in enough miles until I actually started to think I was going to finally dry out. Ain't gonna happen. The next shower was hellacious, filling the roads curb-deep with cold water. It finally got so bad I just tucked my head in and worked my way through the traffic, sightseeing over.

It's a pity, too. I had stopped at a couple places to look around, in the morning before the weather went to hell. Thick green forests, rolling hills, and raucous streams running along the road. I had early dreams of thoroughly enjoying myself in such a pretty place, but not this day. When the rain really starts to strangle, all you see is the car in front of you. And there's always a car in front of you—and usually one behind as well.

So the day went, until I got down below Utica and headed west. I hit a rest area on Route 90, picked up a motel book and found a room along the highway in Syracuse, and finally made my way to a dry place—of course as the sky cleared and the sun came out. I'm sure there are plenty of fun back roads and dirt roads to explore in the Adirondacks, but with all the pouring rain it would have to be some other trip before I'd find them.

The hotel room looked like the aftermath of a rained-out yard sale, with clothes and boots, socks, tank bag and everything else porous draped over the heater unit on the wall. I headed out to find food, hoping for a better day tomorrow.

Ausable Chasm, New York.

20 • One Time Around

7/17/10 Saturday

Leaving Syracuse in the morning, I tried Route 90 for a bit, and decided it was way too thick with death-wish commuters and semis, and opted for NY Route 20 running parallel just a few miles south. Route 20 is a four-lane in most places, carving a border between farmland and suburbia, a nice road; but by ten o'clock the sun was out like a flame thrower, and it was nasty hot for the rest of the day. When I arrived on the shore of Lake Erie I spent some time riding alongside the lake on Route 5, but the heat was way too much and I basically put my head down and went for the finish in my old neighborhood in Amherst, Ohio. Unfamiliarity with the wet vest, and a general loathing of wet, slimy things, kept me from trying it, but looking back I have no idea why not. I sure needed it. I leap-frogged from rest stop to rest stop, buying one or two bottles of cold water at each one and downing them. The only memorable incident was a leather love seat sitting in the middle of Route 90/Route 2 just outside of Cleveland. Always a good idea to keep your eyes peeled for furniture on the Interstate.

I called ahead looking for a friendly place and found it, and spent the night with my old neighbors Jack and Gigi Penton in Amherst, Ohio. 25 years ago—is it really that long?—I lived in Amherst. I had a wife, and daughter on the way, and a good job at motorcycle manufacturer KTM; which was and still is headquartered right in town. I was young and ambitious at the time, and full of good, new ideas; but unfortunately the president of that company at the time did not welcome new ideas, and I soon painted myself into a corner, occupationally.

Oh well. In spite of all the negatives, I made a lot of friends quickly in the area. Some of them are gone now, and things have changed, but Jack and Gigi and I spent the evening telling old stories and laughing, and the time passed quickly. They had somewhere to go in the morning and so did I, so we made it an early night.

At KTM America, Amherst, OH.

Jack and Gigi Penton get ready for a morning ride.

7/18/10 Sunday

My plan was to get out of northern Ohio before the heat settled in for the day, so I left Amherst just after dawn, after checking out my old house, and taking a photo in front of the KTM warehouse. I couldn't help but suffer flashbacks from a former time there. We lived in a small white farmhouse on a big piece of property covered with black raspberry bushes, and could barely afford it while the job with KTM wasn't working out. It was a sad time, except for the birth of my daughter, and very dim in memory since it was a quarter of a century ago. Time heals, though, and a whole lot of shit has flowed through the cesspool since then.

I headed west on Route 2 all the way to Toledo, found my way onto Route 75 and then took the beltway around to 23 north. Not a whole lot happened on the ride. I finally broke out the wet vest after lunch, and it really helped. Made me feel about 20 degrees cooler, and wasn't all that terribly clammy to wear, over a T-shirt. The day also clouded up, and cooled off somewhat without the burning sun.

No incidents. Rode to Route 23 on the northern shore to Tawas City, Michigan. Tawas is a small beach town on Lake Huron, of the classic Main Street/Lake Street/Center Street design. You know the kind—Lake Street would be Highway 23 in this case, with the "highway businesses" on it; a few stores, a McDonalds, a gas station. Main Street comes off perpendicular, and has a tavern or two, a restaurant and more shops, and then Center Street parallels the "Lake Street" and has a few dying businesses on it. Tawas doesn't have a Main Street or a Center Street in it, but the point is, the layout is familiar. As a matter of fact, it would become lots more familiar on the trip, since just about every small town in America shares the same scheme.

Tawas looked tired. And for good reason; it's a summer resort town, and I was landing there on a Sunday afternoon. All the way up Route 23 I had seen the lines of cars filing out, heading back to home and work after partying all weekend on the lakeshore. By the time I arrived, late in the afternoon, the tourists had fled so fast it looked like all the shops had been sucked empty. You see this kind of thing at all beach resorts, ocean or lake, where the proprietors of all the businesses sweep up, restock and lick their wounds until the next Friday, when the hoards descend again. Being a beach lover myself, I've always enjoyed the peace and easy tranquility of a shore resort on a Monday noon, but on this Sunday Tawas looked whipped.

I wanted to stop right in town, so I could walk to food and a little shopping I had to do, but I spent way too much money on a room at a resort hotel in satisfying that misguided urge. This was the first time, and the only time, that I broke the cardinal rule of "motelling it" for the rest of the ride. I waited too long to start looking, was too tired and sun burnt, and thought that this downtown "resort motel" would allow me to walk to a restaurant. A bad decision,

I know. I spent $125 on a room, which, in my mind, is what you might spend for three nights of motel rooms rather than one. After all, you're just going to sleep there. Why would it be worth that kind of cash?

My preference is for the tiny little mom and pop motels; where you park right in front of your door and the room doesn't scream "Corporate designer!" at you. Lots of these places have a washing machine you can use, they're cheaper, the people are friendlier and they need the money you're spending, and will use said money locally. Everywhere I go I try to find the smallest, back-roadsy place, and the more neon in the sign, the better. But this time I ignored my well-proven preferences, and almost immediately regretted it. Worse yet, there was no suitable-looking restaurant within walking distance and I had to get back onto the bike to find a spot for supper. On the way I saw a perfect-looking mom and pop place called the Windmill Motel, just down the highway a half-mile, and I felt like I'd been stabbed. I swore I wouldn't make that mistake again.

7/19/10 Monday

The day started out bad. Fourteen miles down the road from my overpriced room, I realized I didn't have my knife with me. Not a great big deal, not a really expensive knife, but it was my trip knife, and that makes all the difference.

Before I left New Hampshire, I had this thought pop into my head--I should get a knife. I never carry a pocket knife. I also never even imagine myself getting into a West Side Story-style knife fight with a bunch of ne'er do wells. But I knew I needed a knife, so I went out and bought a fairly small Gerber fast-open knife. Nice knife. I found myself using it every day, by the way.

But what is it about guys, and knives? I talked to my neighbor Nate, just a couple of hours before I started the ride. Nate's a cop; he'd pulled into my driveway with the town cruiser. We talked about last minute details for taking care of the house and things, and out of nowhere Nate says, "Do you have a knife for the trip?" I still don't understand it. What is it about guys and knives?

So it was my special trip knife, and of course I turned around and rode back 14 miles to the damned hotel. I hoped it'd be right on the floor of the room, and of course it wasn't. It was nowhere to be found, and suddenly the guy who never carried a knife was feeling totally naked. The whole morning was darkened by the loss of that knife, and of course I couldn't just buy another one. I could have stopped at Wal-Mart and had another Gerber in a second, but I didn't. Somehow or another the next knife was going to have to be provided to me. Spiritually, that was the only right thing. Time would tell if I didn't just go out and buy another one. But I did need a knife. Why is that?

Giving up, reluctantly, on the blade, I continued up Route 23 along the coast of Lake Huron. Route 23 is a typical old-touristy route along the lake, with loads of motels and restaurants, most somewhat time-worn and tired looking. But comfortable. The midpoint of the road is a town called Alpena, which is a substantial town. Road-wise, it's one of those places where the Main Street/ Highway makes a 90-degree turn in the middle of town. Very exciting.

No, seriously, I remember a quite busy main street, lots of shops and people bustling around, mostly in cars. I've always lived in the country, in recent years, and it just seems to me that when people get into towns, most of them won't get out of their car and just walk, even though everything is right there, within walking distance. Instead, you can be riding along a fairly lonely road—Route 23, in this case—yet you pull into Alpena and there's a traffic jam going on. Why not just park your car and do all that shopping on foot? I don't know the answer; I do know that this tableau repeated itself in every town I rode through in America. With few tiny exceptions.

Heading north, after Alpena, the traffic thins out dramatically. Just a lonely ride; me, the bike, and the lake. The left side of the road is wooded, broken here and there by a house and yard, oc-

V-Strom in Paradise—Whitefish Township, Michigan, that is.

casionally, but more often by just a driveway or a dirt road. On the right lies a huge lake, nothing but water to the horizon. The shoreline is sand or rocks, with small waves lapping whatever beach there might be. Out front is a winding asphalt road, devoid of cars, and the picture in the rear-view mirror is the same. The black ribbon reels in from the front, spools under the wheels and unwinds behind. It was a vision that was getting more and more familiar every day.

I stopped for lunch in a little diner in Rogers City, a clean little town a mile off the main drag. The restaurant was the kind of place that most resembles someone's dining room, with a few tables in a converted house, and a staff of local kids virtually clueless as to what might be expected of them in this line of employment. Like maybe they had never been out of town and into, say, a Denny's, so they could see exactly what a real waitperson might do during their shift? After a considerable amount of time I was served a BLT without tomatoes.

My confusion was profound. One would think that the simplicity of the name of such a sandwich would be all that was necessary to convey its ingredients. Bacon-Lettuce-Tomato. Hopefully slathered liberally with mayonnaise, on toasted bread selected according to the mood: white bread if it's a quiet, mellow day; whole wheat, if you're feeling guilty about all that mayonnaise; seeded rye if you're in an exotic mood. But always, the basic construction remains the same. I had to complain. I called the girl over.

"This BLT doesn't have any tomatoes on it."

She looked at me with a pair of big, dewy eyes, reminiscent of the photos of baby harp seals back in the day when suburbanites were still pretending that they cared about what Eskimos chose to have for lunch.

"Oh... sorry," she said, genuinely concerned, but still somehow confused at my dissatisfaction. "did you want some tomatoes?"

I said yes, and she eventually brought out two slices of tomato on a dish, and apologized again. She still appeared confused, but not nearly as much as I. Perhaps she'd never actually seen this most common American diner menu item in her brief 16 years on this planet? On the other hand, maybe I had strayed into a part of the country where they prefer their BLTs without tomato? I remain confused to this day, but the road was calling, so I bid adieu to Rogers and their BLs.

All the way up towards Cheboygan the road rolled by, and a sense of loneliness rolled over me. I couldn't shake the feeling, and it made me uneasy. It's one thing to be alone, but quite another to be consumed with loneliness, and I was definitely feeling the blues. Being alone on this trip was the choice I'd made, and I had no regrets at this point. When you have riding partners you always have to compromise—your destination, your pace, your whole philosophy. You can't do your own thing because your partner or partners always have a different goal. I wanted to do exactly what I wanted, on the spur of the moment, wherever I wanted to do it, and so far that part of the trip was working out fine.

Could be it was just the silent, huge lake on the right side, gray and calm and reaching flat all the way to the horizon; too smooth and quiet for an ocean, and all the more unsettling because it didn't smell salty. Maybe it was the empty Monday afternoon road ahead and the drone of the 650's tires on the tarmac. Could be it was just me, wondering what the hell I was doing way up on a lonely road in Michigan five days into a ride that had no real purpose, and no fixed idea of an ending. And maybe I was just lonely.

I stopped and walked down to the shore of the lake and sat down to think it over. It was a beautiful day. Light rain showers from the morning had cleared away to a partly cloudy afternoon, and it was no longer roasting-hot, just great, warm July weather. There were a number of places I was looking forward to seeing on this trip, but no place I'd rather be than here right at this moment, looking at something brand new and looking forward to plenty more of the same. I dug out the peanut butter and some crackers, a bottle of water, and enjoyed the moment a little longer. I watched the loneliness melt into the lake, and just felt alone and content again.

Mackinaw City was the top of Michigan's lower state, and from here I had to cross over to the Upper Peninsula. Crossing the Mackinac Bridge was a real event. I took a few pictures on the south side and then hopped on, into a traffic snarl that had us crawling across the bridge at about eight mph. Not the kind of speed the 650 Suzuki likes to travel. To make matters worse, the right lanes were closed for construction, and the left lanes are metal mesh. If you're on a bike, and you look down, you can see right through the metal mesh like you're looking through a window screen. The lake is seething away down there about a jillion feet below, and it looks like you're falling.

Now, I don't suffer from a fear of high places, but the view below made every hair on my body stand on end, which in places is an awfully odd feeling. I snapped my head back up to front and center, but then had to look down again as my skin crawled. I have to admit that I felt as if getting off the bike and laying down by the side of the road would feel really good, but it just wasn't possible in a construction site traffic jam on the third longest suspension bridge in the world.

Instead I took a few moments and lingered at the rest area on the north side of the bridge. Walking to the restrooms I passed what was obviously an "Iron Butt" rider's bike, a Yamaha FJR with a massive custom-made fiberglass tank where the passenger seat would have been. On the way back out I chatted with the rider, whose name I didn't get. A quiet talker, obviously a loner, like the rest of us, I guess. He was out for a "quick ride," which as far as I could tell would cover about 6000 miles over the rest of the week. He wasn't the last long distance rider I'd bump into during my trip. Where I was interested in riding around and seeing things, these guys seem only to want to ride, and the farther they can go and stay longest in the saddle, the happier they are.

The world changed completely on the other side of the bridge. Northeastern Michigan, lower peninsula, might be somewhat rural, but the Upper Peninsula is totally rural. I had dallied enough at the bridge that riding farther was cutting into my down time, so I left Route 2, the coast road on the Lake Michigan side, and rode north, inland, to find a motel. The first place I had picked out from a magazine at the bridge, but it not only had no internet, it also had no cell phone service. Which I didn't want to give up just yet.

So I went to the next town, and along the way a sign of potential trouble with the bike appeared. A red idiot light came on, and "FI" initials lit up in the small display on the Suzuki's dashboard. Obviously, the "FI" had something to do with fuel injection, but whatever reason the light would come on was a mystery to me, as I'd never read that page in the manual. If I even had a manual. The bike still appeared to run fine, and I wasn't about to cut the bike off and sit there by the side of a lonely road in the middle of critter country. Without any smoking or bucking or death-rattle sounds, I continued on at 70 mph to the intersection I was looking for, and

Tahquamenon Falls, Michigan.

then stopped to figure out what to do. The bike was idling steady at 5000 rpm, no desire to go lower, and I debated shutting it off. It may not have started again.

There was a small restaurant across the street, a place where I could get other people involved if I had to, so I shut it off just to see. Start it up and it ran and idled fine, no red light, no "FI" indicator. I rolled over to the restaurant and asked for the nearest motel, which was just three miles up the road. If I'm going to have a sick bike, I can deal with it in the fullness of the morning. If it seems fine, I ride, and deal with whatever comes.

The waitress's instructions pointed me up the road to a specific motel on a corner that happened to have two motels, a couple hundred yards apart. "Don't go to the other place," she said, "trust me." She was right; this was my kind of place. The Gateway Motel in Newberry. A small place, maybe ten or eleven units, parking right up front. Folksy room with a box fan rather than air conditioning, a book shelf full of books and magazines in the room. Small television on an antenna, certain to only pull in three or four local channels. Clean and tidy, and only $35 a night. If the bike didn't work, I could see myself staying here for a few days.

My room was next door to "Buffalo Chip" Rich and Cathy, his wife, from Vancouver, Canada. Rich and Cathy were both comfortably fleshy in middle age, full of humor and the easy-going attitude that is so common in Canadians and so rare in this country. I got myself settled and then met them again for dinner at the local tavern, and had a jolly old time solving the world's problems. But it's awful hard to get a feel for what's happening in America by talking to Canadians. They're just worried we won't go broke and take them with us, or finally just start bombing them because they're an easy, close target.

7/20/10 Tuesday

In the morning I rode from the hotel to Tahquamenon Falls, near Paradise. I had to. If I told anyone I was only 23 miles out of Paradise and I didn't go, it wouldn't make any sense. I arrived in the town of Paradise at about 8:00 in the morning, and it was a sleepy place. Not much happening at all. There was a café open, though I'd already had breakfast. The travel information center had an "open" sign out, but there was no one there available for conversation, so I kept moving.

I had no bike trouble on the way to Paradise or the falls. The bike could have been acting up because I had filled it up at the first town past the bridge the day before, and maybe the gas was a little punky. I had tipped in some StarTron fuel additive the night before, and let it be. I had no trouble all day, as a matter of fact. It seems that the "FI" indicator and the red light is just one of those endearing computer glitches that show up on modern bikes and cars. I checked the internet for any explanations for it, and figured out how to "hotwire" the fault code readout on the V-Strom's display. There were no fault codes in memory, so if whatever was happening wasn't throwing a code I figured it probably wasn't any kind of real trouble.

Tahquamenon Falls is one of the typical attractive wild areas in this country that have been surrounded by a fence and "preserved." Not literally. But there is a gate to check you in and clean restrooms and souvenir shops and snack bars, and there's actually a micro brewery within the park. The falls are very impressive; an upper and lower falls, loads of water flowing through. I spent some time chatting with a Forest Service girl there, and happened to mention that I hadn't seen any police cars in many days, and I thought that was a little strange. She told me about a mileage restriction on the police cars, meaning that they're not allowed to drive all over creation. I guess that's why I hadn't seen them on the road. Also that I should be doing 60 to 65 on the roads, that at 55 they'd all run me down. All valuable local knowledge!

Local speeds concerned me, because I just wasn't in a hurry. I had been falling into a rhythm with the V-Strom, and it seemed that it liked to be ridden at a lazy 60-65 mph, or even less, so that's where I'd been most comfortable. I am not a speed demon, and I had already decided that I was in this for the long haul, so there was absolutely no reason to rush anywhere.

After the falls I got back on Route 28 and headed west. Route 28 is a great road. Two-lane, rolling, low traffic and fun, even though it's the shortest distance east to west across the U.P. I had also escaped the summer heat; as a matter of fact I was bundled up with the electric vest on half the time.

My destination for the day was Duluth, Minnesota, to Aerostich Manufacturing, a major manufacturer of motorcycle clothing and riding accessories--the people who created the Gore-Tex clothing I was now comfortably wearing every day. I planned to spend a couple days visiting with my friend Andy, who is the principal shareholder in the company, and in order to get there before nightfall I had to keep on rolling. I realized right away that I had set a goal for the day, and in doing so I had to hurry to make it. The thought that here I was ignoring the scenery and rushing down the road crept in once again, so I stopped for a cup of coffee and a sandwich on the shore of Lake Superior once I rolled into Wisconsin. I swore I'd forget about deadlines and just ride to please myself from that moment on, but it was a hollow promise since I knew there was another deadline to meet on the other side of Duluth.

There were some showers in the afternoon in Wisconsin that couldn't be avoided, but they weren't bad. I was surprised by the change in time zone, and disappointed that it added an hour of riding time to what the GPS was telling me. The GPS knew I was going into Central time, but it didn't tell me 'til I got there. It's a Garmin Nuvi 255W, and I refer to it as the "Evil GPS" because it has its own ideas occasionally about what would be an entertaining route. Since I also owned an old Garmin GPS176 I had them both mounted on the handlebars, an arrangement I came to really appreciate and probably will never change. The old 176 is waterproof, and has a

Aerostich Riderwear, Duluth, MN.

screen that is easier to read, and it just sits there and tells me exactly where I am. The Nuvi is better for finding things—like Mexican restaurants—so it gets used for all the navigation chores.

The Nuvi is also excellent for finding out where to stay at night. I very quickly fell into a ritual every evening. Once I decided where I thought I wanted to stop, I would pull over and tell the Nuvi to find all the motels in the area. I'd pick the most likely-looking and, since the GPS had the phone number right on the screen, I would call each motel and check out the price and whatever amenities I might be looking for—restaurant across the street, laundry room, internet service, whatever. Then, I'd ride into town to check out what I like to call the "neon factor" and make a final decision. The neon factor tells you just how cool-looking the motel is, which makes a big difference in your state of mind. Especially if you're spending more than $35 on a room; which happens all too often these days. Using these methods I hoped to avoid ever walking blind into a $125 a night "resort hotel" and feeling stuck there.

I learned something interesting about the V-Strom and what kind of fuel it likes earlier in the day. With a range of about 200 miles to a tank, I was filling the bike twice a day, at least. I'd tried just about everything in the tank so far, with mixed results. But, in Wisconsin I came across a prize. I stopped at one gas station that had 103 octane racing fuel, with no ethanol in it. Hot damn! Up 'til now I'd been suffering with varying degrees of ethanol in the fuel, and the added alcohol didn't help the way the bike ran at all. Now I'd get a chance to try rocket fuel, and I eagerly filled the tank with it.

What a terrible mistake. I don't know if the bike was pre-igniting or if the fuel was just so slow-burn that it couldn't get it together in the Suzuki engine, but it wasn't good. The exhaust note changed, the engine made rumbling, moaning noises out the exhaust, and power was down by a good ten or twenty percent. I rode carefully on that tank for about a hundred miles, then stopped and filled the bike with ethanol-enriched crap regular gas, and the bike finally started running healthier. Within another week of riding I came to the conclusion that "Plus" grade fuel was the best the Suzuki needed—it didn't like Premium—and for the most part plain old low-octane Regular was fine. Tip in a little StarTron and the bike was happy as pie.

It was a great feeling to arrive in Duluth. I had been there once before, in town for the World Observed Trials round that happened at Spirit Mountain, many years before. After hearing about Aerostich's Very Boring Rally and not being able to go there at the time, I swore next time I'd arrive in Duluth on two wheels. And here I was. The first objective of the trip was accomplished.

I went to dinner with Andy and his friend Ken, who is a college professor teaching creative writing. Same exact field my sister is in. We had a great time and good conversation, and a few margaritas at a Mexican place right on the lake.

One of our topics of discussion was the decline of western civilization, as we see it at the end of the first decade of the new century. We agreed that, specifically among single males of our age, we can blame most of it on women locked up in cars, talking on cell phones (to other women), pejoratively profiling men on the outside of the cocoon they've built. In such a case, there is no contact between the two subjects; and upon making a quick decision that the subject male is scum because he doesn't have the right shoes, phone, car, clothes or other material devices needed to transmit the idea of unlimited cash on hand, the subject female quickly speeds away, and there is no hope for the mating ritual.

As a second example, say you, the free-wheeling freedom-loving motorcyclist, happens to be walking down the neighborhood street, and you are approaching a little boy playing on the sidewalk. You notice he's playing with a toy truck, the exact replica of one you played with as a child. So upon approaching him you say, "Hi little boy, that's a neat truck you're playing with!" Chances are, before the mother even arrives on the scene the police will be there, and you will do well to not be led away in shackles. We are profiled constantly, and we live in a land of fear and mistrust. We cheerfully decided that there was no hope for society, and parted satisfied with our mutual good company and conversation.

Parked at the headwaters of the Mississippi.

7/21/10 Wednesday

First rest day of the trip. Spent time at Andy's just relaxing, and working on the bike. Needed a half quart of oil, chain didn't appear to need adjusting. The bike appeared to need nothing at all, although the tires were wearing. The bike also seemed to be running better the more fuel I ran through it. Quite possibly, since I bought the bike used and it had been sitting for a while, just riding it was flushing out fuel system sludge that had accumulated with time. I "hot-wired" the display and read no codes on the ECU again, so the FI warning the other night must have been a momentary glitch. I decided not to worry about it any more.

The zip-up vinyl holder I'd been using for the Garmin Nuvi claimed to be waterproof (which the Nuvi isn't), but stitching seams along the zipper and top window did indeed leak in the storms. Andy gave me some seam sealer, so I did my best to seal everything up a little better.

Which made me wonder why most every tank bang on the market isn't waterproof also, right from the box. Instead, they're made out of leaky nylon packcloth with a zillion seams, and in order to keep water out you have a separate flimsy "condom" that pulls over the bag and is supposed to protect it. Well, I was using a Chicane tank bag on the V-Strom, and for reasons deeply rooted in aerodynamics the wind gets under the rain cover and blows it right off the bag at even moderate highway speeds. There was no way to keep the rain cover on unless I pull out a one-inch clinch strap and wrap it around the bag and rain cover and cinch it into place. This, of course, makes it impossible to get into the tank bag with any amount of grace. One day I hope to own a tank bang that fits well, holds what I want, and is totally waterproof without any help.

Other than working on the bike a little, I took it easy all day. Which actually was necessary, since the Mexican food we had the night before went through me like Drano. Ah, the joys of being on the road! When Andy got off work he took me on a two-wheeled tour of the city, and we actually stopped in front of the house in which Bob Dylan was born. How about that?

Duluth is an appealing little town—in the summertime—but closer inspection reveals some threadbare spots in its regal robes. Local belief is that Duluth was a major rival for Chicago, when the Westward Expansion was going on, and the short end of the story is that Chicago won. Duluth was a bustling little town of the Paul Bunyan flavor at the end of the Civil War, overflowing with natural abundance that was easily commercialized. Timber logging and lake fishery kept everyone employed, and fortunes were made. Copper and iron ore caused a land rush there in the middle 1800s, and though Duluth's fortunes went up and down, by the end of the 19th century it was a thriving town.

By the beginning of the 20th century Duluth was the major northern port for the United States, and it was the home of millionaires and the playground for the rich and famous. The Industrial Revolution brought steel and shipbuilding, and the town continued to prosper. Then, in the 1970s, it all came crashing down as U.S. Steel closed its plant, and Duluth's shipbuilding and heavy machinery industries followed in big steel's footsteps. Tourism eventually came in as a partial balm to the wounds left by failed industry, and much of downtown is very appealing in a café, shops and restaurant kind of way. But, the rest of the city still shows the common scars that come from a sudden lack of livelihood. Poor neighborhoods rub elbows with tattered mansions in this town, though by my experience the people are friendly and will go out of their way to make you comfortable.

Dylan's place of birth is a peach-colored, two-story, nondescript house in a working class neighborhood. The Zimmerman family is said to have rented the upstairs rooms of this two-unit dwelling at the time young Robert was born. There is definitely nothing remarkable about the place; and it's interesting to reflect that in Dylan's autobiographical work he implies that his first impression of northern Minnesota was a feeling of not belonging there. As tired and bleak as some of these tattered neighborhoods may appear, I'm sure that the majority of Duluthians are quite happily located and will defend their town in any debate. In the summertime, that is. You might be able to crack their resolve in mid-February.

7/22/10 Thursday

It was Thursday, July 22, and after hearing from some friends in New York, I knew I had to be in Pueblo, Colorado, on Tuesday, the 27th, to meet them for some riding. I now had a schedule again, my worst enemy. But what price comes from trying to be a social animal? I knew most of this ride was going to be spent alone, and my friend Gino was riding out from New York City with a friend of his, and neither one of them had seen Colorado before, or any of the American West. I would have the opportunity to show them around a little, and gain the benefit of some entertaining riding partners for at least a brief period of time. I knew that Gino was a good company, as well as a very entertaining fellow. I trusted that his riding buddy would be the same.

So, looking ahead to all the ground I would have to cover between Duluth and Pueblo, I got an early start. I headed west on Route 2, looking for Route 200, as suggested by Andy as a fine two-lane road that goes from about 50 miles west of Duluth all the way to Idaho.

First though, it was time for food. I had breakfast at a restaurant near the Spirit Mountain exit on Route 35 south of Duluth, a place I'd been to during the international trials about six years ago. I had a fun job for the past 25 years, and actually even before that, one that took me around to all parts of the country, and actually the world. So it's possible for me to be in Duluth, Minnesota, and suddenly realize I know where I am, and know where to get breakfast. It gets even better on the West Coast, since I lived there for eight years at one point. I was heading into a few states I'd never traveled in before—North Dakota, South Dakota, and Nebraska—which was an exciting prospect. But in the mean time, it was comforting to know that if I took Route 35 down to the Spirit Mountain exit there was a diner I'd been to before. A tiny bit of local knowledge helps you feel at home just about anywhere.

I got settled in the diner, and immediately was greeted by a retired truck driver at a nearby table. He was sitting with his wife, having breakfast, and looked as if he'd already tired out the other few tables there, and turned his attention towards mine. We spent the next half-hour chatting back and forth across the room. Without a doubt, climbing off a well-packed bike in the parking lot, and trudging inside shedding a huge pile of riding gear marks you as a wayfarer, and I'm sure he was searching for some sort of kindred spirit. "I spent 50 years driving truck all over this country," he said, "and never saw any of it. So my wife and I sold the house--couldn't afford the house and a camper--and we bought a trailer and now we camp everywhere. We're going to spend the winter in Texas, already have a nice place reserved. I got a nice 30-foot camper, that's all we need."

He had plenty more to say about all the great places they'd seen, but he sounded like he was trying to talk himself into it. Both of them looked tired to me.

I have to admit, I have a disturbing ability to absorb vibrations off of people, and though I don't understand it very much, most of the time I feel like people near me don't even have to talk and I'm already feeling what's going on inside their heads. I say disturbing, because it's not a very comfortable thing, most of the time. Yeah, I know, it sounds like bullshit. But my girlfriend at the time would probably back me up, and swear that most of the time I already knew what she was thinking. Of course, maybe that's just self-preservation, on my part.

This couple didn't strike me as happy, at all, and their company that morning, though welcome, was bringing waves of depression over me. Mr. Truck Driver had a look of panic in his eyes, and his wife barely looked up at all. What's the truth of it? Are they doing this out of choice, or had it really come to the point that they couldn't afford a house, and figured they might was well wander around and see some things; spend some time being tourists before they settle down into homelessness? I don't know, but I do know that the vibe was intense and disturbing, and I carried their company with me for a few more hours after I got back on the road. We're living in troubled times. The dollar isn't worth anything anymore. The investment houses and insurance companies are taking everyone's retirement funds away, and loads of people are mortgaged up to their eyeballs. Maybe I just had a brush with the walking wounded, which naturally makes me wonder if I'm just another one of them.

I snapped out of it suddenly, when not far into that morning's ride I crossed the Mississippi River, at a spot where it was barely 30 feet wide. Of course I had to get off and take a couple photos. From this point on I was officially "west of the Mississippi," and it felt good to be there.

Route 200 turned out to be a good road. There was no traffic at all until I pulled over at a major crossroad and two semis and four huge campers got in front of me. It still wasn't a big deal. The land is flat and everybody stayed close to 65. But when they did slow down it was nasty to ride in the dirty air behind them. Dirty air, meaning turbulence. On a bike, and maybe especially a small bike like a 650 V-Strom, the dirty air knocks you around like a punching bag. The Suzuki already has an airflow problem, evidenced by the number of them on the road with aftermarket windscreens, and also that annoying habit of shedding the tank bag's waterproof cover. Get behind a big old motorhome—and if it wasn't going too slow you would have never caught up to it, right?—and your lazy afternoon scenic ride is suddenly fouled up.

I finally had to pass them all, one at a time, when the going got a little hilly. And it was unnerving. The 650 does not have an excess of horsepower, and passing someone who is hovering around 50 mph is a project, once you're finally trapped behind them. Because of course the road is twisty and hilly; if it wasn't they'd be flying down the road. Uphills force a re-calculation of what gear you want to be in and how much room you have to reach terminal velocity, and downhills are a problem because you start wondering about what kind of speed you'll be doing when you reach that curve that's only a quarter-mile ahead. Keep in mind that whatever speed you'll be doing, you will also have a careening motorhome right behind you, piloted by a guy who now wants to show you how well he can drive at speed. Either that or daydreaming about how much fun it would be to just mow you down and leave your bones in the ditch. You can never tell these days.

So I did the stressful thing and passed them, one by one, each "passee" presenting its own unique problems in accelerating and overtaking. When I got out into the clean air again I stayed in passing mode for while, until I had a safe half-mile on them.

And then, of course, I crossed the Mississippi again, south of Bemidji, Minnesota, and just had to stop for another photo. I didn't even bother looking up. I could feel their looks.

Here the river was so narrow that you could wade across it in two steps, and upstream was a wild-looking swamp. I've seen this river so many times down south, in and around St. Louis, where it's the muddy, "mile-wide" Mississippi of Mark Twain's days. Such a huge difference between that and the creek I was standing next to. I was at the headwaters of the Mississippi, and if being "west of the Mississippi" hadn't sunk in at the earlier crossing that morning, here was the end of the argument. On the other side of this ditch the Great American West began, and it would be thousands of miles before I saw this river again. I dallied there for a while and let the campers get some distance on me.

Where my rest day was all sunshine and clear skies, this day was back to business as usual. As the day progressed the thunderclouds grew. I had looked up the weather channel in the morning, and saw where the big storms were going, and I had a more or less clear path, or so it seemed, in the general direction I was heading. That didn't mean I would stay dry. That just meant that when I rolled into a storm I had faith that it would peter out before it got any worse, and I was more or less right.

Luck started running out on the far side of Minnesota, though. I dearly wanted to get to North Dakota before stopping for the night, and I had been staying dry for the past hour, and really wanted to keep it that way. Route 200 was looking wet ahead as I approached a crossroads, and I had to make a decision. North to Grand Forks, or south to Fargo? I wouldn't have minded seeing either of them, but I wanted a straight shot as west as possible to the other side of the state, so I turned north instead of straight into the storm. My idea was to head to Grand Forks, a fairly large town, because I was still paranoid about the "FI" error, that was occasionally recurring, and I also had started hearing a clicking from the back of the bike.

I may have made a mistake. The storm followed me on my left side, and of course I was moving quicker than the storm. I turned left onto Route 2 towards Grand Forks, and started feeling drops. I pulled into a truck stop for some coffee. Took the computer in too, just in case they had wifi, which they did. Weather.com showed two massive storms--12 hours or so later these same storms would combine to drench Wisconsin and close the airport in Milwaukee, as well as delay the start of the Oshkosh air festival. I saw a gap between them, or I thought I did, so I headed back out onto Route 2.

Two miles down the road I knew I'd made a bad mistake when I crested a slight rise and saw a wall of water about a half-mile away, right across the highway. I pulled an immediate U-turn across the median, then a right turn on a gravel county road heading south. I wicked it up to about 70 mph on the gravel, not real comfortable on the relatively smooth highway tires. Ten miles down the road another road intersected, so I turned right and sped down for another ten miles, effectively doing an end-run around the tail end of the storm. I came back up to a soaked and puddled Route 2, but I was still dry. And mighty proud of myself.

Grand Forks was a busy, bustling strip-mall of a town, lots of speeding traffic and confusion. I had the GPS tell me where the motel district was and headed there to find a room. The clicking/clunking coming from the back of the bike was getting louder, and it sounded ominous. After a lot of investigation later on it turned out to be noises coming from a dry chain. I guess the chain doesn't

Mississippi River, Jacobson, Minnesota.

like high speed in the heat, followed by soaking rain. I would have to get more chain lube and hope that will help it.

Parts are coming, though. I have Pete ordering me a new set of cush-drive bumpers in Colorado, and Lucy is meeting me there, bringing my replacement tires and a new set of brake pads. All I have to do is keep the bike together until Denver and all will be good.

I can't say much good about Grand Forks. After riding across the lonely prairie all day, it was a huge shock to suddenly be jammed into six lanes of huge pickup trucks at rush hour trying either get home two minutes ago or kill someone trying. I used the phone and GPS to find a fairly cheap motel, then found an even cheaper one right around the corner. No mom-and-pop places, just chains, and I had to park way outside behind the building and couldn't watch the bike. I pulled out a black nylon bike cover I had packed for just this purpose, and when I was all done unloading I wrapped the 650 up for the night.

There were no little diners or restaurants anywhere around; again, they were all chain establishments. The first place I walked into was jammed full of screaming children. The cheerful young hostess greeted me loudly, and I backed right back out the door. The next place was a steak restaurant chain, promising at least a 45 minute wait. Holy cow, don't these people know there's a recession going on? I finally wedged into an empty seat at the bar and ordered a beer or two, and had my dinner right there with a noisy baseball game in front of me. By the time I got back to the motel I was itching to get to sleep, just so I could get up early and get out of that town.

7/23/10 Friday

When I was packing the bike in the morning, I had the unintentional company of a woman dressed in pajamas with a rag tied over her head. She was sitting on a bench next to the back door, apologizing for her appearance but she needed a smoke. She said, "Are you really from New Hampshire? Wow, that is cool. Long way from home."

She volunteered that she was from Fargo, and was in town because of some kid's sports endeavor, I really wasn't listening that closely. Said she'd grown up in that region her whole life, never even seen the east coast. I asked her if farther west the land started turning to prairie land, and she looked at me like I had a hole in my head. She had no idea what I was talking about. "What's a prairie?" she said.

I rode out of Grand Forks worried about the noises the chain was making. It was a crunching, snapping noise, the likes of which I'd never heard before. I thought the wheel bearings were disintegrating or something worse, but I stopped at a Napa Auto Parts for chain lube and the noise disappeared. At least now I knew where the noise was coming from. Somehow I thought that an o-ring chain would be indestructible on a street bike, but I was slowly learning differently.

I decided to continue on Route 200 because it had been fun so far. It was a mellow day. Nothing much was happening in North Dakota. Route 200 runs straight as an arrow through these parts. I had the GPS set for a town on the other side of the state, with the preference on Route 200, and after a few twists and turns the GPS said 160 miles 'til the next turn. It was hardly exaggerating. The first half of the state was farm fields--soybeans, canola, corn, all money crops--and quite flat. The hills were building to the north and south though, and I looked forward to what might happen ahead.

I stopped for gas in Bowdon and chatted with the guy at the gas station. Nice guy, early sixties. Pleasant and friendly. Talked about farming in the area, lack of rain and such. He looked at the storms coming and indicated that I'd probably get caught in it.

He was right. This day, the rain came in on gentler, slow moving thunderstorms, like it was fixin' to stay a while. It's not as exciting as a tornado-toting, green-sky slam-banger of a storm, but you still get wet. I looked around along the way for a motel, didn't like much of anything I saw. By the town of Hazen I had had enough of riding in the rain. It seemed like I was getting to where an hour of braving the thunderstorms was about my limit. It was fairly late in the afternoon anyhow, and I needed to do laundry. Although the rolling plains of North Dakota are beautiful in their own way, there wasn't much happening in the way of scenery.

One interesting place was Garrison Dam, but unfortunately as I was approaching it the weather turned foul. The thunderstorms were building early this day, and rain made a photo of the dam impossible. I did get one good shot of a lonely church alongside the road before the downpour began; after that any kind of sightseeing was pointless.

I stopped at the Roughhouse Motel in Hazen, where I was surprised by the time zone change again. When I stopped, I thought it was about four in the afternoon, and the clock over the desk at check-in told me it was barely three. "Is that clock right?" I stupidly said to the guy at the desk.

"Yep. You changed to Mountain Time right at the county line."

And the county line was about a quarter mile away. That explained my confusion when the GPS found the motel, and then told me I'd arrive there a hour earlier than it already was. One of these days I'll figure it all out. The Roughhouse was a nice place, free coffee 24 hours a day, laundry room, internet, cable TV. I spent the afternoon washing all my clothes and getting up to date with e-mail and such. And I got to spend some time watching the Tour de France, which was a rare luxury.

Apparently, there was one restaurant in town. I followed the desk clerk's directions to a Main Street that was a few blocks south of the highway. Putting Main Street way back in a corner of town, when the highway came through, was a typical move back in the day when cars were starting to take over the landscape. It keeps the town's main drag quiet and peaceful, which at the time is exactly what the townspeople wanted. And it worked; Main Street remained unspoiled, and the new highway—Route 200, in this case—carried all those noisy cars efficiently past on the outskirts of town; or in Hazen's case, between town and the northern "suburbs."

The trouble with this plan is that it was too effective. Once traffic was routed around the town, nobody stopped to spend money. The new fast-food chain restaurants and gas station/mini marts go up alongside the highway, where they get all the traffic, and the end result is the slow death of all the downtown businesses. Hazen seemed to have enough local support that some of the old businesses are surviving, but farther on in the west I would see this trend repeated with disastrous results.

I found the local eatery, and had high hopes when I saw exactly how homey the place was. In most towns, this kind of place is the place to go for home cooking, but not in Hazen. The food was terrible.

I fell into talking to an old guy at the town restaurant. He was impressed that I came all the way from New Hampshire on a motorcycle. He laughed and said, "What do you do when you get caught in the weather?" I just said, "Keep on riding!"

I also stopped and chatted with a local state cop running a radar trap on a side road. He knew the bike I was riding and said earlier in the year he rode his street bike all the way around Lake Superior. All the short conversations I have indicate that folks seem to be real nice around here, and out on the road it's obvious that there's a lot of motorcycle fans in this part of the country. I had been getting waves and thumbs-up signs from people driving cars. Everybody seemed very friendly, which is a stark contrast with the way a motorcycle stranger might be received on the East Coast.

Without exception, everyone was amazed to see someone from New Hampshire on a bike, crossing the country. It kind of hurts a

Mr. and Mrs. Rotobale, somewhere in North Dakota.

little when people hear I'm from New Hampshire and you see they have to scratch their head and think for a bit to figure out where it is. Without a doubt, there are very few New Hampshire license plates in this part of the country, on bikes or cars. I got into a quick conversation with someone at a gas station who saw the license plate and commented that he may have never seen a New Hampshire plate in that gas station before. I laughed and told him that was because most folks in New Hampshire can't afford to leave. It makes a good joke, but I also know how true it is.

Chased into Hazen by rainstorms, terrible food and a time constraint all helped me to temporarily forget that I was finally crossing paths with Lewis and Clark, the intrepid explorers who blazed a route from St. Louis to the mouth of the Columbia River in Oregon 200 years ago, back before there was a Subway at every truck stop. I knew I had passed a sign pointing towards the site of Fort Mandan, the Corps of Discovery's first winter camp, but at the time I was being drowned while trying to find the motel. In the morning I had my mind set on a remote breakfast spot, because I wasn't interested in trying my luck at the only game in town again. So I left Hazen in the wee hours, and completely forgot to check out Fort Mandan. You see? You miss a lot when you're in a hurry. I would see more of the Lewis and Clarke expedition later in the trip, much more, so it wasn't that great of a loss, really. It would give me an excuse to ride back some day.

7/24/10 Saturday

I packed everything up at 7:00 in the morning, but didn't make it five miles out of the motel before the bike decided to quit. Actually, it didn't quit completely, but it was running terribly, with no power. It appeared to be running on one cylinder. I nursed it up to the parking lot of a John Deere dealer on the edge of Hazen, and started the diagnosis. I didn't want to take anything apart, because the V-Strom is at best an annoying machine to work on. You have to take off the fairing shrouds in order to do anything on the bike, and each shroud has five bolts and numerous plastic snap connectors holding it on. I schlepped around for a while fiddling with things that obviously weren't broken, and then got out a set of hex keys and got to work.

With the shrouds loose and the tank lifted up, I removed the fuel line, moved everything out of the way and hit the key. Gas squirted in a long stream across the parking lot. I knew it wasn't a fuel injection problem though, because if it was the computer would have kicked a fault light on. So it had to be electrical, and it had to be a spark plug, if not a bad coil. The rear plug isn't that hard to get at, and I pulled it out and looked at it. Not a problem with it, but I replaced it with a spare I had with me. To get at the front plug, I had take another four bolts out to pull the radiator off, but luckily the hoses could stay connected. As soon as I could get my hand around the spark plug lead I knew what the problem was.

I had my friend Brian, at Eddie's shop back home, pull the bike apart and check the valve clearances before the trip. I told Brian that while he was in there he might as well replace the plugs for me, and he did. But then he routed the spark plug wire wrong— which is easy to do--and there wasn't enough wire length to really seat the plug cap. I re-routed the wire, shoved the plug cap all the way on, hit the starter button and the 650 roared to life.

For the first 3000 miles of the trip, that spark plug cap had been just barely touching the tip of the plug, and it had taken this long to finally break contact. Honestly, I'd just as well have it happen on a foggy early morning in Hazen, North Dakota than lose power on a freeway near Detroit. I started the task of bolting everything back together, and all tolled it was about 45 minutes lost.

Meanwhile, the sunny, bright morning clouded up, and I was sure I was about to get rained on again. Luckily I never did, though I passed through a couple of dense fog banks later that morning. This was the first day in a while where the thunderstorms held off, but it was cold all day, even in the sun. I wore a T-shirt and a long sleeve T-shirt, plus my electric vest, and if there wasn't a problem with the wiring I would have turned the electric vest on at one point.

The vest wiring was my only dumb move, and a pain in the behind. I wired in a separate circuit for the vest and routed the wire alongside the feed for the pass-through into the tank bag (I had a pigtail inside the tankbag so I could re-charge my phone, iPod, camera, whatever). I wanted to make all this wiring bulletproof, so I used some stout heat-shrink tubing to lock it all into place. The thing I didn't count on was the stress of bending that well-protected wire at exactly that spot every day, because I had to un-clip the tank bag at the front of the tank and then flop the tank bag onto the seat to get at the gas cap. It takes about 20 seconds to fill the tank, then I flop the tank bag back up, re-clip it and I'm off.

Well, it worked for a while, but I used crimp connectors on the vest wiring and all this flopping back and forth, sometimes three times a day, broke the wires at the crimp connectors. I had no vest power; and though I knew exactly what had gone wrong, I had made the setup so well-protected that there was no graceful way to get in there and repair it. I did have a second vest plug available for a passenger, but it was buried under the seat and so far I had resisted fishing it out and using it. Hey, it was late July, why should I be cold? The time would come when I'd finally fish it out of there and have to use it, but like the body-cooling wet vest, I was fighting off the urge. I must be a lot lazier than I appear.

So I had left town without breakfast, vowing not to go to the lousy cafe from the night before. I figured I'd just hit the first place in the next town. Well, each town along the way had a cafe or restaurant, and all of them were shuttered and closed down, testimony to the country's economic collapse. I wound up riding 100 miles to a little restaurant on Route 85. That marked the end of my ride on Route 200, which served me well over two states. I knew that 200 goes through Montana and Idaho though, so I was hoping I'd see more of it later in the trip.

This day was a lot of grassland, and a lot of grain fields of one type or another. By the time I got out to the National Grasslands on Route 85 the landscape had turned hilly, a welcome break from

Well, it's the sure-enuf center of the country!

the flatlands preceding it. The only interesting diversion was a 32 mile gravel loop I took south of the town of Redig, looking for the geographical center of the United States. It was a good road through pastureland, and I was able to keep the bike at 60 through most of it. Gentle rolling hills, green as can be, rolled off as far as the horizon. The sky was bright blue with white clouds—the clouds presaged what storms might chase me later on—just an absolutely gorgeous day. If I stopped there was no noise, just whatever sound the breeze might make, rattling through the grass. Every now and then I passed a lone antelope, standing on the side of a hill watching me ride by. Wrapped up in blue and green, on a good bike, buzzing down the road on a warm afternoon in the northwestern corner of South Dakota. This was exactly what I was looking for, when I started this ride. This was my bell ringing, if I can borrow Ken Kesey's phrase.

I have to stop and point out the myth of long-distance motor-cycling. If you spend any time searching out and reading all the cross-country tales of other motorcyclists, you can be lulled into thinking that long-distance cycling is like riding through utopia in a euphoric haze. Nothing could be further from the truth. Most of your time on the bike is spent trying to find the right route, avoiding the storms, finding the correctly-placed gas station, dealing with things on the bike that aren't exactly right, trying to shift your weight so the hot spot on your rump doesn't turn into an angry welt, thinking about food, dealing with traffic, looking for a great place to stop and get a drink; and if you're one of the unlucky ones (or unskilled ones) nursing along a bike that is shedding parts or working its way towards complete failure. Or, like a number of long-distance motorcycle hero tomes I've read, actually trying to learn how to ride the bike while you're circling the globe. These moments when everything clicks into place and you get to enjoy your surroundings are actually somewhat rare, and it improves your trip to a great extent if you're able to recognize these little shreds of euphoria when they come along.

For a few miles I rode alongside an antelope that had no choice but to run with me in an attempt to get away from me. I had no idea that antelopes can't jump, and this one was stymied by a pasture fence following the dirt road. Eventually I backed off and let it cross into open prairie on the other side of the road. That antelope had no trouble maintaining a steady speed of 40 miles an hour while I was pacing him.

The center of the nation is marked with a cairn alongside the dirt road, and a flag deeper into the field on the other side of a barbed-wire fence. I'd imagine the flag is the actual spot, but I was close enough right where I was. Back where I come from, tall grass means ticks and chiggers, and I wanted to avoid crawling bugs if I could. I took a picture and kept going. Grasshoppers and birds shared the road with me, and I wound up wearing a number of the grasshoppers. None of the birds here hit the bike, but I had killed a bird earlier in the morning on the paved road. Every now and then they'll swoop out and make contact; the one in the morning hit the fork tube on the right side of the bike. Another good reason to wear a helmet.

All these roads through the grasslands are two-lane, and it's not uncommon to come across a highway worker in the middle of the road with a STOP sign, and you'll have to shut it off and wait for a while, sometimes as long as fifteen minutes or so. Then a pace truck comes along leading a line of traffic coming the other way. The truck turns around, the opposing cars clear out, and then you have to follow the pace truck through the construction site. This happens fairly often, and creates an opportunity for conversation if anyone else gets out of their car.

North Dakota countryside.

At one stop for construction work I met a guy driving a van, who claimed to be a former motorcycle race mechanic. We chatted about bikes for a while, and I asked if he was still in the business. No, he was working for a gun shop now, and he was delivering ammo to a Cowboy Action shooting match, apparently being held up ahead somewhere. After we continued on for a while I started thinking it'd be pretty cool to find the match and watch it, but I turned off at the wrong spot and lost the ammo guy, and had to miss it. I stopped for the night in Belle Fourche, South Dakota, and I was glad to have a room fairly cheap. I was told the prices were way higher down the road in Sturgis, so I decided to stay north of the famous motorcycle town and instead cruise through on Sunday morning.

I realized this day that I was nine days into the ride, with 2879 miles on the clock. I could vaguely remember ever having a job, and was starting for forget what my house in New Hampshire looked like. Nice! The only trouble I noticed was an increasing sense of fatigue, which was surprising me. Years and years of riding and racing dirt bikes had convinced me that just riding around on a street bike couldn't possibly tire me out. But I was quickly learning differently. The stop in Duluth had been much-needed, and here I was only a couple days out from a day off the bike, and I was already tired. Clearly, there was much more to this than I thought.

7/25/10 Sunday

I started out the day with breakfast in Belle Fourche (pronounced Bell Foosh), listening to ranchers complain about all the grasshoppers. I knew about them. I was still wearing a lot of them.

This day seemed like a touristy sort of day; I spent most of my time cruising below the speed limit just looking around at things. I rode down to Spearfish, South Dakota, looking for the Spearfish Canyon Highway, since I had heard it was a cool road to ride. In town I passed a Dodge camper van for sale alongside the road and had to stop to look at it. $3500, Runs Great! That's just about what I could get for the bike. Maybe I'd be back if things didn't work out.

Along with a passport and credit cards, a main item in my survival kit was the title to the bike I was riding. I packed this along because I figured if I had trouble bad enough, or got tired enough of all the riding, I could sell whatever was left of the bike and find another way home. It would not be unreasonable for me to find a cheap motel in a medium-sized town, take out a Craigslist ad and sell the bike, and then blow the money on a used Dodge camper van and continue the rest of the ride on four wheels. Or take a bus. Or get on a train. Or even buy a plane ticket and find someone to pick me up at the airport. This is also not the sort of thing that you usually read in someone's book about the Ride of Their Lifetime and how it was All About The Ride. I knew from the beginning that I didn't care if I came back on the bike or not, and here in the first half of the ride that was still quite true. For me, it wasn't All About The Ride. It was all about poking around in the far corners of our country, and if the bike turned into a pain in the ass, I was all set to dump it and walk if I had to.

The Spearfish Canyon road, 14A, was a great ride. The speed limit was slow, but Spearfish Canyon is a tight little canyon and very scenic. High rocky walls fence in an amazing amount of greenery, with a pleasant little river chasing alongside the road. There's a motel and bar right at the Spearfish entrance to the canyon that looks really cool. At the other end is the town of Deadwood. I couldn't help but laugh about it, after watching the HBO series "Deadwood," which was purportedly about this town and its inhabitants in the late 1800s. It would be hard to imagine. Deadwood is pretty much a modern casino town now, so there's no easy place to park, what with the tourists and gamblers, and no place to just stop and get a cup of coffee unless you enter a casino. I've been in casinos all over the world, and they all look the same. I figured I'd just stay outside and enjoy South Dakota instead.

Deadwood is a curious place, in that you can't miss its namesake. The hillside above the town is peppered over with dead trees; bare husks sticking painfully out of the ground, like something from a Dali painting, and nothing living short of sparse grass to break up the tableau. It's really a stretch of the imagination to think that those same dead trees were there more than a hundred years ago, to give the place its name; but here in the arid west things dry out and hang around a while. Back home, nothing lasts much more than a decade before the mossy damp eats it up.

I went up to the graveyard and paid my respects to Wild Bill Hickok and Calamity Jane. They are interred next to each other on the side of a rise overlooking the town. I didn't know much about them, honestly, other than they were colorful figures from a time I find a very difficult task to imagine. Cowboys and Indians? Gunslingers and outlaws? I thought it was something all created by Hollywood, even as a kid. Yep, I grew up thinking everything was created for television. But here they were, planted in a real place with their names etched in marble. The cemetery was full of locally historic figures I wasn't familiar with, but it was peaceful and quiet, as you'd expect to find a graveyard. It was hot and dry. Really hot.

Since I found myself among strangers, I did what most people do any more. I found a bench to sit on, a weak signal for the cell phone, and called my girlfriend.

I drained my water bottle back at the bike, but I was still jonesing for another cup of coffee. Hard to believe it could be 90 degrees out and some damn fool would want hot coffee to drink, but us addicts are wired differently. I finally stopped at a snack bar/gas station outside of town and found my fix. Two other riders were there on sport bikes, so I went over and said hi. They were both on barely legal canyon chargers, basically home-built roadracers with a minimum of street-legal fluff. They kind-of looked at me, in all my Gore-Tex, and my fully-loaded touring rig, and kept their cards close to their chest. This motorcycle life is so weird. We wave to each other when we pass on the road, but up close we're all split into factions that try their damndest to avoid contact with each other. Generally, I was finding it easier to get into a conversation with someone in a Subaru full of kids than with one of my own kind. Sad but true.

In spite of our perceived differences, I managed to pry a few words out of them. They did say I oughta be glad I'm not here in town in two weeks, when Sturgis bike week is happening. One guy simply said, "It sucks." They said every square inch in every town, up and down Route 90 and all the local roads, is packed with bikers and people. I'm not sorry to be missing it.

After the coffee break, I headed down Route 385 to Mount Rushmore, which was a tangle of cars and campers. There are toll booths set up at the observation point, a huge parking lot with six lanes of toll-takers, getting ten dollars a car. It didn't look like much of a bargain to me, so I just snapped a quick picture and kept going. Came back around and down to Hill City for some lunch, then followed 385 to Custer. In Custer they have a Crazy Horse monument--same system, four lanes of toll-takers asking for money. The project officially started in 1948, and so far they have Crazy Horse's face cut out of the rock. I was thinking it was going to be a while before they finish it.

Leaving Crazy Horse, I headed south on 385 to Hot Springs, then kept going down to Chadron, Nebraska. It had been hot out all day, and I was just about wore out enough at Chadron to stop for the night. I almost stopped, even started checking up on motels. But I looked at how far I had to go the next day and decided to ride down to Alliance, 50 miles further on. Another 50 miles, even at the end of a long day, is not that big of a deal out here. It was basically a straight line between Chadron and Alliance, which would take no more than 45 minutes, really. Of course, in typical fashion I rush out onto the road again before looking at the gas gauge, and then turn around and fill the bike before continuing. It's never a good idea to head into another stretch of boondocks without a full tank.

My first choice of motel in Alliance was full. Hard to believe. I would have thought everybody driving around in Alliance, Nebraska, on a Monday night would be close to home. The motel manager steered me towards another place, owned by a friend of hers, and she promised me it would be cheap and nice. She was right, it was decent.

Upon unpacking and getting my daily notes down, I noticed on the map that Alliance is home to Carhenge. Now here was definitely a sight worth seeing, and as it turned out I was only a few miles south of the site. As sunset came down, I rode out to Carhenge to check it out. It's a spot where some enterprising soul has reproduced Stonehenge in scrapped car bodies, and painted them all silver. Admission to Carhenge is apparently unregulated. After avoiding the ticket-takers at Mount Rushmore and Crazy Horse, getting to see Carhenge for free made my day.

I was glad to have the chance to see such a sight in Alliance, but I only wound up here because time was catching up with me. I had to be in Pueblo, Colorado, the next day to meet my New York friends. I had a rough plan for two-wheeled sightseeing with them, but I only had one day to do it. After that I had to high-tail it to Sedalia, south of Denver, and meet my girlfriend for five days of rest, off the bike. So this day and the next I would be rushing through the landscape, although there admittedly isn't a whole lot to see in southern Nebraska and the Great Plains of eastern Colorado. Not to say I'm bad-mouthing it, though. I like the open spaces and wall to wall sky in this country. But, as I've said before, it's more fun to be moseying around rather than hurrying somewhere.

Carhenge, Alliance, Nebraska.

7/26/10 Monday

Alliance, Nebraska, to Pueblo, Colorado, was a series of straight-line shots through increasingly hot, flat, boring country. One section was "78 miles with no services." Early in the morning I veered west towards Scottsbluff, stopping to look at Chimney Rock along the way, and snoop around their visitor center. Signs around the building warned of rattlesnakes in the area, and please stay on the sidewalk. They don't have to tell me twice. I was well away from Lewis and Clark's wandering this far south, but Chimney Rock was a well-known landmark on the Oregon Trail as the "emigrants" moved west in the mid-1800s. You're actually riding on pieces of the Oregon Trail when you turn your wheels onto the dirt roads in this area, but at this point in time there's no danger of getting cross-rutted in wagon tracks. Stopping to see what it looks like now, and standing back and surveying the vast countryside is a good way to remind yourself what a rough-ass thing it must have been for the pioneers to cross this country originally.

The temperature was up to 99 degrees when I finally reached Pueblo, where I would meet Gino and Alberto for the next day's ride. I rode to the other side of Pueblo and found a Mexican fast-food place, where I bought a couple of tacos and about a half-gallon cup of iced tea. I wanted a beer, or two, but I couldn't afford the laziness that would come along with it. I wasn't sure how much farther we had to ride to get to our destination, but I did know that I was pretty much baked dry and exhausted already.

Through the miracle of cell phones I connected with them easily enough, and we rode together the last 50 miles to Westcliffe. There we met our friend Gregor's father Bob, who helped us out finding a room and a bike shop. We stayed in the Courtyard Country Inn B&B in Westcliffe, a delightful place. It is an old motor lodge of the "courtyard" style, with the rooms decorated just like someone's country bedroom. The courtyard was planted as a flower and herb garden, along with a fountain and a chiminea that already had a fire burning for us. We arrived late enough that the only place available for dinner was the bowling alley, and it was the best bowling alley food I've ever had.

The heat finally left us on the last 50 miles up to Westcliffe. The temperature dropped at least 30 degrees as we moved up onto the Front Range. Westcliffe is at 8000-plus feet, and you can feel it after coming up from the lowlands. But they're not so low, really. The ride from Alliance never saw an altitude much lower than 4000 feet, and I was surprised that the GPS reported elevations of 5000 feet and above in the Colorado farm lands below the Front Range. Even so, it was a hot ride.

After nearly two weeks on the road, it was fun to have company. My friend Gino came from Italy only about 19 years ago, learned English and his way around New York City, where he now owns a fine restaurant. I'd met him through mutual riding friends a few years back, and liked him immediately. He is the owner of a huge sense of humor and a quick ear-to-ear grin, and he can make "macho" a joking matter in the way only a true Italian can. His best put-on is a readiness to fight at all times—as in, if he doesn't understand something you say, his response might be, "Are you making fun of me? Because I'm Italian? Really? Because if you're making fun of me I have friends I can call who will make short work of you." It is impossible to explain this in print and get the point across; I wish I could send you to a YouTube video instead. Suffice it to say time spent with Gino is time full of belly laughs, posturing and posing.

Alberto was new to me, although his parallels with Gino's history were almost identical. Alberto is from Mexico, also spending time in New York and somewhat new to the language. He was quieter than Gino—most people are quieter than Gino—and a good straight-man to Gino's antics. They had both ridden from New York to Colorado in two days, which is an average of 900 miles a day, and though they should have been exhausted they were both boiling over with enthusiasm for their trip. I knew they'd be excellent riding partners for the next day.

After such a broiling hot day, it was kind of comical that we were sitting in the courtyard of the motel, quietly talking about the next couple days of riding, around a merrily burning chiminea. Like we needed the extra heat. Our hosts had left a few random bottles of beer on ice, and some wine, and though we did our best the three of us were worn out entirely. It was one of those evenings where I wish I had the stamina of a 20-year old, but I couldn't stay awake. We slept that night in eager anticipation of getting farther into the cool mountains the next day.

7/27/10 Tuesday

My New York friends had new tires put on in the morning, making for a late start. Bob had taken us to a bike shop on the edge of town, and we waited in the morning sun as the mechanics changed tires on both the bikes. I would have plenty to do on my bike, but in a few days I would stop for a week's rest and have time to devote a whole day to maintenance. On this day, all I did was top up the oil and wait for the other guys.

Gino was riding a KTM 990 Adventure, while Alberto was on a BMW 1200GS. Both of their bikes were brimming with every conceivable accessory and add-on you could imagine. In addition, they had ridden out from NYC with their spare tires lashed across the top of their aluminum panniers, in true desert explorer style. Without a doubt, either one of them could furnish anything you could ask for out of their voluminous packs, if they only knew where to find it. With most of the gear removed for tire changing, the parking lot of the bike shop looked like an especially interesting yard sale. I felt grossly under-packed in comparison, but I also felt like I didn't need to be carrying anything more.

It was good to lay around in the sun, in the cool air that comes with a little bit of altitude. I wish I'd had a lawn chair. The thought occurred to me that with all this touring and riding, I still hadn't even noted my mileage down in my calendar. A lazy glance at the odometer proved that I had put on about 3500 miles so far, but I seriously wasn't counting the miles. It did seem like a long way to ride, but I also knew that in a month's time 3500 miles would be insignificant. And I still wouldn't be keeping accurate records.

In every other long-distance book I'd read, the writer always kept detailed notes of mileages between here and there, total mileage, how many miles before breakfast, and so on. Especially, the reader would be regaled with minute details on exactly what sort of miles-per-gallon the rider was enjoying, whether the bike was going uphill, downhill, with a tailwind or headwind. I could honestly say I hadn't bothered to check. All I knew is that the fuel gauge would start blinking somewhere around an average of 200 miles, and I'd have to stop and buy more gasoline. On the ride from Alliance to Westcliffe I had stopped for gas three times, and it made me tired just to think of it. But soon the boys were finished, and we broke camp at the bike shop and rode our bikes into the Rocky Mountains.

We rolled up from Westcliffe to Route 50 and then turned left, heading way uphill. After the heat of the day before, it was a thrill to top out at Monarch Pass that morning while being pelted with wet snow. We were officially high in the Rockies now, and for the time being we'd leave the oppressive heat behind.

Basically we rode from Salida to Gunnison to Montrose, pausing to look at the scenery along the way and stopping at a good Mexican restaurant outside of Gunnison for a leisurely lunch. We were going to head down Route 149 to Lake City and Creede, but a nasty-looking thunderstorm in the area changed our minds. Instead, we rode down into Montrose, all the while watching huge, black thunderheads form, seemingly all around us. The weather was boiling up from the south-southwest, and we were looking at a wall of greasy-looking green-black clouds, right in our path. We stopped alongside the road into Montrose and regrouped. My riding partners were enjoying their first ride through Colorado so much, I didn't want to stop at a chain motel in Montrose. My plan was to take them up the hill into Ouray and spend the night in a real cowboy town. We checked the maps and the GPS, and it looked like when we turned south to Ouray there'd be a chance we could outrun the storm that was definitely heading our way fast.

We got on the road up to Ouray, and it was obvious we weren't going to beat the storm. It looked more like the storm was going to beat us. I noticed we had passed a 4-H fairgrounds with a huge open-sided livestock barn, and I also noticed the gate was open. A half-mile farther up it was obvious we were going to get pummeled by rain, hail, and who knows what else, so I spun it around and led our small group through the open gate, into the fairgrounds, and right into the barn, just in time to avoid 20 minutes of hammering precipitation.

This was a skill I had been developing since Michigan. The key is to keep your eyes peeled for open barns, canopies, self-service car washes, garden sheds, any place that could provide shelter from a fast-moving thunderstorm. You can never know what might be up front, but if you know in the back of your head that you passed a self-service car wash just two miles back, it's simple to spin around and make a run for it.

It's not about being a sissy, either. I don't mind riding in the rain at all, but when a 60 mph wind hits you, along with cold rain and hail, you do tend to imagine many places you'd rather be. And one of them is not a rain-filled ditch, or under the wheels of a speeding tractor-trailer that didn't see you. We were happy to just cool it for a half-hour under cover, just 'til the worst had passed.

Phone calls to Ouray confirmed that the rain had stopped there, and also reserved a couple rooms for us at the Ouray Hotel. We were also warned to be careful, as the town was clearing up the debris from a flash flood that swept the road we'd be riding in on. Good thing we stopped. On the edge of town we rode through the mud that still covered the road, and saw the pile of rocks the bulldozers had already pushed out of the way. Add "landslides" to the list of things you avoid when you seek shelter from the storm.

We putted into town in a lingering light rain, and checked into the historic Ouray Hotel, built in 1893 and dominating one corner of this charming little cowboy town. The guys were blown away. You see, neither one of them had seen anything of the Olde West before riding through Colorado. True, you have to be able to see past the gift stores and souvenir shops and recognize the bare bones of the town, and see it for what it once was, but both of my friends were easily capable of this. If you don't pay attention to the commercialism, which of course is necessary to maintain any kind of local economy, Ouray really is a pretty little town.

We walked Main Street before being pointed to the Western Hotel and Saloon for dinner, as a place the locals would be more inclined to go. We settled into the tavern, with its fine old walnut bar complete with stuffed animals and a huge painting of a happy and topless belle from many years before. Beers were poured and steaks were ordered. We weren't disappointed, and passed a fine evening there, though mighty tired.

Gino and Alberto in the Western Saloon.

7/28/10 Wednesday

In the morning we rode from Ouray to Silverton for breakfast, on one of the most impressive highways in Colorado—the Million Dollar Highway. Both of my riding partners were stunned by the scenery, and they would be extremely jaded if they weren't. The name "Million Dollar Highway" is lazily applied to the road between Ouray and Silverton, but originally the name referred to a 12-mile section of the road, Highway 550, that crawls over Red Mountain Pass from Ouray. There's a bit of dispute on how the road got its name, but it's generally accepted that the lofty title came about because it cost a million dollars to build in the 1920s. Comical to think that it'll cost more than a million to just think about building such a road these days.

The MDH is a great ride on a bike, though it can be a white-knuckle experience for some in a car. Riding down it that morning, I couldn't imagine what the experience must be like for the drivers of those huge motorhomes that dominate the vacation highways. I heard one local joke that "Colorado ran out of money when it came down to guardrails." It must be true, because this high-dollar two-lane road is completely absent of them, and it will raise your heartbeat, even on a bike, if you get distracted by the view for just a second. The roadbed twists and turns up over the pass, and you'll come around a curve and have a breathtaking Rocky Mountain vista in front of you just at the same time you realize you've just wandered out of your ideal line a few inches. If someone's coming from the opposite direction you might feel every hair on your body stand up tall. It's a good road to stop and enjoy the view. Tough to sightsee while you're rolling along.

We had breakfast in the Avalanche Cafe on the far end of Silverton, on the suggestion of one of the locals. This morning was an ideal example of what kind of great times you can have just by being open and receptive while you're on the road. So we took this guy's advice, and went to the Avalanche, where he and a couple of his friends also came in for coffee a little while later.

We got to talking, and Bruce and his friends were interested in the bikes and our riding adventures so far. So as it turns out, Bruce was also a local sheriff on his day off, and he owned a brand-new Kawasaki KLR650. While talking with him, I could see the gears turning in his head, and finally he admits he's itching to take it out and put some miles on it. We had been discussing dirt-road possibilities for riding out of town, and finally Bruce volunteered to ride his new KLR up Ophir Pass with the guys, if they wanted to go. Well yeah, that sounds like fun!

My day was already decided; I had to head back to Sedalia to meet Lucy, and it was past time for me to leave. So while Bruce ran off to get his KLR, I said my goodbyes to Alberto and Gino, and we agreed to try to get back together later in the week when they were on their way back.

This is a beautiful corner of Colorado, and one that deserved to take up more of my time, but once again I had made plans and had to flee the action. The guys went on to follow Bruce up Ophir Pass and down the other side, and then, while Bruce rode home, they took a spur of the moment run out to Moab, Utah, just to see the place.

I left at 10:30 and had a non-stop eight-hour ride to get back to the meeting point in Castle Rock in time. It was a hell of a day. I rode from Durango to Pagosa Springs to Del Norte, and then up towards Salida, pretty much only stopping for gas. It was pretty typical. At times the road was open and I could maintain a good speed, and at other times I was mired in local traffic. The one thing about Colorado, though, is that the scenery is always awesome.

When I got somewhat closer I let the GPS tell me the short way there, hoping to save 50 miles or so. The Evil GPS picked back roads that initially looked great—small paved roads winding along following the creeks and such. Soon the paved road turned to finely graded dirt—still excellent. But then the dirt road turned into a smaller dirt road, then suddenly into a two-track. Nothing terrible, mind you—it would have been rotten if it was raining. But it was dry, and I kept going. Soon the dirt road turned into an ATV trail; I even passed a sign welcoming me to a certain ATV riding area.

This was starting to get ominous. The two-track turned into a singletrack trail, but it kept going. I finally came across a guy in a jeep, who was somewhat surprised to see a guy on a fully loaded "touring" bike, this far back in the dirt. I asked him if the path I was on would finally come out onto a paved road up ahead.

"Well, yeah. It will. But not for a while..."

He started giving me directions, which is a useless thing for anyone to do. I have to see it on the map, and I scrolled the GPS ahead to where it appeared that things would get better. Of course, while this was going on, the afternoon clouds were building, and the last thing I wanted was to caught on this hardpack trail surface once it started raining.

"In other words," I say, after he drones on with directions for a few minutes, "if I just stay on this I'll eventually find my way to civilization, right?"

"Well yeah, you will."

That's all I needed. A few miles ahead the ATV trail emptied out onto a dirt road, where a young couple on a four-wheeler watched me go by in awe. The dirt road was the right road, according to the GPS, and although the surface of the road was like marbles on a glass-topped coffee table, it was going towards the right place. Soon enough I was back on pavement, and then on a beeline to the restaurant in Castle Rock where we would all meet. Lucy, my girlfriend, who was coming in from Arkansas, and my friends Pete and Lisa, who lived nearby. I arrived about 45 minutes ahead of Lucy, and all was well.

7/29/10 to 8/2/10

The next five days were basically rest days, off the bike. And it was necessary. I come from a dirt biking background, lots of off-road racing for years, some of it particularly grueling. When I started this trip, if you would have told me I'd eventually find myself exhausted from riding a street bike on pavement, I would have laughed in your face. I knew I was tired when I arrived in Duluth, and was happy to take a day off. But, by the time I got to Sedalia, after lashing my way through thunderstorms and cold in the Dakotas, then searing heat, then freezing mountain passes and a quick loop of Colorado in two days, I was absolutely beat.

I wouldn't laugh about it any more, but I'm still amazed at how fatigued you can get just tooling down the road. I took extraordinary pains to set the bike up just perfectly. I could get on it in pitch black, with my eyes closed, and the handgrips will wind up being exactly where they need to be—no pulling on the bars, no forward hand pressure on the grips. Perfectly neutral. The grips are big, fat Sunline touring grips, without a doubt the biggest grips I've ever found (not foam grips, these are rubber), and they're so fat I can just wrap my hands around them, which is great because I've got big hands. Skinny grips make me feel like my fingers are wrapped twice around the bar, which is a nasty feeling when your finger joints are eroding with arthritis.

A larger than stock Givi windscreen on the V-Strom does a great job of keeping most of the wind off, and handguards keep the rest of the wind from blowing up my sleeves and flapping me to death. Finally, an Aerostich sheepskin seat cover keeps my rear end happy—and without a doubt I would never leave home for a long ride without that piece of sheepskin. I tried a few different seats before I left, finally settling on the combination of the Suzuki accessory touring gel seat and the sheepskin pad. A month later in the trip I would ditch the gel seat and buy a Sargent World Sport seat for the final 1500 miles, but then sold the Sargent seat on Ebay when I got back because I wound up not liking that, either. But the sheepskin pad remained through it all.

The bottom line is, this bike was perfectly comfortable; about as good as you can get for something you're going to be spending eight or ten hours a day riding. In spite of that, riding it wore me flat out. I parked the bike carefully in Pete's garage and didn't even look at it for three days.

Instead we got in the car, and toured around. Along the way we met up with Gino and Alberto again in Aspen, and they were tired also, but enjoying the hell out of life. They had ridden down to Moab and taken an easy loop on their bikes, then came back up to Colorado to see what Aspen was all about. From there they planned to maybe ride up to Steamboat, then across through the Rocky Mountain National Park before racing back to New York to get to work on Tuesday. Madmen!

Lucy was really patient with me, as I pled exhaustion, but she wanted to take a ride on the bike. Originally, we might have planned an overnight to Leadville or something, but I whittled her down to a day trip to Cripple Creek and back.

Things are a lot farther apart in Colorado than you might think. The distance might look short on the map, but the roads wind around enough to double the apparent mileage, and I knew she wasn't ready for what she was asking for. What she got was a typical short morning on the bike, for me. We headed down towards Cripple Creak, starting out on dirt roads—dicey, with two people aboard. We stopped for coffee, then stopped for lunch, then finally got within striking distance of Cripple Creek when a thunderstorm I'd been watching decided it was time to head in our direction.

We stopped at a scenic overlook, and I pointed out the storm to her, plain as day, heading straight for us—or us into it, depending on which way you looked at it. An occasional fat raindrop was already falling. I gave her a quick rundown on what it was like to get drenched on a bike, while I removed the sheepskin pad and put it in the topbox to keep it dry. "We can either go forward, and put up with the rain, or turn tail and run. Your choice," I told her. Smart girl. She picked the "cut and run" option, and we got out of there and headed north, quickly. I took the longer way around to avoid the dirt roads (no fun in the wet), and we scooted back to home base. In all, we had ridden a bit shy of 200 miles, and she was just about screaming for mercy by the time we got off the bike. "I don't know how you can do it!" she told me, knowing I'd been averaging four hundred miles in a day, or more. I guess the short answer is, you've got to have a screw loose somewhere.

The next day we took a ride to Boulder, us on the V-Strom and Pete and Lisa on Pete's BMW 1150GS. We had lunch in one of the many bars that dot the landscape in that college town, and had a fine afternoon. On the way back, my tormented chain finally gave up the ghost and broke a master link. I'd been listening to it start clicking again, and when the click turned into a clunk I pulled to the side of the highway quickly to check it out. The fixed side of the master link's sideplate had snapped in two, and luckily I stopped before the chain separated. It's not like I wasn't expect it, eventually. So I pulled off the seat and dug out a pair of pliers and a new master link, and had it fixed by the time Pete and Lisa missed us and turned around.

I know a good motorcycle touring story is supposed to be full of struggle, and seemingly insurmountable problems with the machine that have you being dragged back to civilization in the back of a turtle truck, but I'm afraid the reader is going to be disappointed with the rest of this tale. Other than this one small problem with the master link, and the plug cap popping off in North Dakota, I had no problems with the bike. No flat tires, no overheating spectacularly in the middle of nowhere, no bike breaking in two, no crashes, and never even running out of gas. I'm not boasting when I say every ride I've ever taken has been like this, it's just plain fact. Oh, I've had odd things break in my life, but never anything that I couldn't easily fix or get out of painlessly. And that was the mechanical story of this ride, if not my entire life. Nothing went wrong, the bike was almost flawless. Not exactly action-packed reading, but it's true.

Lucy headed back home on Monday, and I hung around an extra day to work on the bike and get ready for the next stage of the trip. I had Pete's shop put on a new Dunlop 606 front tire, and borrowed a car to drive there and pick up some oil. The bike also got a new Sidewinder o-ring chain and new EBC brake pads, both had arrived in the mail courtesy of my neighbor, who had dug them out of my garage. I also gave it an oil change and filter, and installed new cush-drive blocks that I had ordered when I first heard the chain noise and mis-diagnosed it as worn out cush drive parts. I also repaired the break in the wiring for the front heated vest hookup. I didn't have the parts, nor the inclination, to fix it properly, so all I managed to do was cob it back together for a while. I'd need to fix it again before long.

I also bought one extra DID master link after having all the trouble with the first chain, and packed it with the other two links in my kit. I'd only had a hint of it so far, but the chain was going to be the weak link in this excursion, no matter what I did. I had read about chain-line problems in the V-Stroms before I left, and spent hours measuring and aligning, and I know I had the sprockets lined up perfectly. Even now you could rotate the rear wheel and check the rear sprocket carefully, and there wasn't a sign of any side wear on the sprocket; none at all. But, I had just eaten up a chain that had hardly 6000 miles on it.

It was only the first chain of the trip. This second chain, an excellent-quality Sidewinder o-ring, was only going to last 6000 miles as well, and by the time it had gone all the way to the back of the adjusters I had a theory firming up in my mind on what was going on. This trip convinced me that you don't want an o-ring chain on a street bike. Why? Because as it spins, the chain gets hot. The summer heat makes it even hotter, and as it spins merrily for hours on end, every molecule of lubricant that started out in the chain follows the laws of centrifugal force and gets flung off the chain. When you get out the spray lube at the end of the day, you can spray as much of it as you want on that chain, and without some sort of force in the opposite direction there's no way to get that lube past the o-rings. What happens is, within two or three days of solid riding you've got a basically dry chain. The surface lube you spray on it helps somewhat. But it can't save the inside of the chain from certain destruction.

Wyoming thunderstorm.

The master link is the "weak link" for sure, and that's where it'll break, eventually. When I installed the new chain I lubricated the inside of the master link with Never-Seize and good waterproof grease. I even packed a small tube of Never-Seize and re-lubed the master link with grease a couple weeks later. Every time I popped a master link off it was dry and galled, no lube anywhere in sight, regardless of all the spray lube and the special attention with the Never-Seize. I'm convinced now that the only chain to use is a non-o-ring chain. Without the o-rings you at least have a chance to get lubricant back into the chain. I'm also thinking that maybe the on-board lubing kits sold by some of the aftermarket companies may be a good idea for really long distance riding, as long as you don't use an o-ring chain. An auto-oiler would be messy, but you don't ever want your chain to break on the highway, or out in the middle of nowhere. Or at all, come to think of it.

8/3/10 Tuesday

I left Colorado for Wyoming, fairly early on a Tuesday morning. The first stop was an IHOP in Castle Rock, and there I made the decision to take Route 25 all the way to Fort Collins, just to get around the city quickly. I soon found out that Route 25 was a traffic jam all the way into the city, with no real through-roads around the problems, so I crawled and suffered into Denver. I took 287 north out of Fort Collins, and it was good to be back in the prairie again. Clouds building off of the mountains turned into a threat after the Wyoming line, and I started trying to outrun the worst storms again. I took a side dirt road that was posted everywhere with "Private Road" signs, and finally chickened out and went back to the main road. On a whim, I got on Route 80 east from Laramie, running right in front of a nasty storm. In Cheyenne, I stopped at the Sierra Trading Post outlet to duck the storm, shop, check the weather on the computer and see what the hotel situation was. There were so many clouds to the northwest in the mountains, just where I wanted to go.

I considered staying in Cheyenne, but the weather radar showed a hole I could possibly slip through and go back to Laramie, so I tried it and succeeded, taking just a little sprinkling while the blue curtains of rain poured down on either side.

You gotta love computers. I was carrying an Asus "netbook," small and light, zipped inside of a leather book cover; well, a bible cover, I guess. Aside from allowing me to take notes easily and hold all the photos I was taking, it also helped with navigation and what little bit of planning I did. Of course, by now the iPhone and clones are the accepted standard for web browsing and navigation, but the iPhone doesn't have a keyboard and tons of photo storage and probably wouldn't have been all that satisfying for me. But, every place you go, out on the road, has a wifi connection available, and I used that computer every day.

It used to be, a good motel had color TV and a pool. Now, if it doesn't have an internet connection I pass it by. Modern times.

I found the Hotel 8 in Laramie, right off the highway and right next door to a nice Mexican restaurant. Had a margarita that must have been 16 ounces, the full capacity of a mixing tin. I wobbled back to the motel afterwards. Alcohol definitely eases the pain of riding, and also the agony of being alone again. But it was good to be back on the road and moving the trip forward.

8/4/10 Wednesday

I walked outside my motel room tonight and was just a little surprised to see a four-point buck strolling past on the sidewalk. It was especially surprising considering that my motel is in the center of Thermopolis, Wyoming, Broadway and Sixth Street, the busiest intersection in town. I walked past the small diner on the corner in front of the motel, and came back around to find the deer eating the leaves off a small tree on the sidewalk, partially protected by a wire wrap. I guess they wrap the trees for good reason. The deer wasn't too comfortable sharing the sidewalk with me, so he moved off across Broadway, at a very leisurely pace.

It was kind of a slow, lazy day anyhow. I left Laramie fairly early, after breakfast at the diner and a fun give and take with one of the waitresses. I've always liked waitresses—old-style waitresses who are flirty and call you "Hon." It makes a travelin' man feel welcome. I used to joke that pretty waitresses and female bank tellers were my favorites, because one of them is giving you food, the other money. Ah that life could be so simple.

My short-term plan, at this point, was to head north to Yellowstone. I had no long-term plan once again, which felt good. From Laramie the natural path would have been to book it up Route 80 for 75 miles or so and then head north on Route 287. But, a spur of Route 287 covered the same distance by looping north out of Laramie and then to Wolcott, about an hour and a half ride with a couple of photo stops. The rolling plains scenery was great, and the road was virtually empty of other vehicles. It's always so strange, to leave a busy mess like Route 80, full of speeding 18-wheelers, tandem trailers and cars, and find a local highway with nobody on it. What a perfect situation if you're on a bike! And then, rolling back towards Interstate 80 at the end of this loop, I can see riders on touring bikes going by on the superslab. What in the world are they thinking?

I came out of the loop and went up to Rawlins and stopped at a diner at about 10:30, very interested in a cup of coffee and a piece of apple pie. But as I was shedding my jacket I noticed a looming black mass to the west. Figuring the wind direction, I could see it was headed right towards me, and fast. I took a look at the storm, looked wistfully at the diner, and then decided to outrun the storm. Maybe there'd be pie up ahead.

I skipped that storm easily enough, but after a couple hours of riding another confrontation was brewing right in front of me. The landscape was incredible. Small rolling hills and fallow fields or grazing land as far as the eye could see. Gold and green, and a blue sky up above, plus the billowing black-bottomed clouds growing in the northwest, as usual. Up in this country you get a chance to watch and contemplate the storm for a while, try to decide what sort of move it was going to make. This one was black and ugly, with a huge anvil-shaped wall cloud right in the front. I watched it fascinated as I rolled straight towards it, and started getting a little nervous after 20 minutes of not seeing any kind of shelter. Nothing but golden fields and the road out front, but the GPS did show some sort of a point of interest up ahead a few miles.

I was still on 287, north of Jeffrey City. I drew nearer to a fork in the road, and the GPS wanted me to go east-northeast on Route 135, which looked to be a collision path with the storm. Staying north into Lander didn't look like much of a bargain either, and after a few minutes waiting there, it was obvious there'd be no avoiding this one no matter what I did.

Fortunately the mark on the GPS turned out to be a rest area right at the crossroads, Sweetwater Station. The rest area had brick and concrete structures protecting the picnic tables; I noticed that right off. Looking around, I also saw a little open shed in a utility yard across Route 135. Nothing else close by offered much in the way of shelter for a motorcycle. There were no real amenities inside the rest area, and I wondered if there might be a place with shelter and coffee a short ways up the road.

It was a typical situation for me, paralyzed with indecision while I tried to find the best temporary accommodations. But when the wind started seriously picking up I got on the bike and jumped the curb, and rode it right up over the manicured grass into one of the picnic table shelters, squeezing between the table and the concrete wall. I shut it off, removed the sheepskin seat cover and high-tailed it to the protection of the rest area building with about 15 seconds grace.

From the inside of the concrete block building I watched as the wind howled like a hurricane. A trash can blew by, followed by a few tree limbs and the odd chunk of bush or two. The rain and hail hammered down for about 20 minutes, and then it was over. As soon as the rain stopped I trotted over to the shelter and eased the bike back out, lest someone think I wasn't supposed to be parking there. A half-hour after it all started, it looked like it had never rained at all.

But playing tourist all morning, and the unplanned thunderstorm stop, put me way behind in what I'd planned to do during the day. I stopped in Riverton for some lunch, then decided to head up to Thermopolis and probably stay there, since it would be approaching five o'clock by the time I arrived. Checking out the billboards on the way gave me some ideas for some off the bike distractions, so I started checking the GPS for motels.

I had a fine old time strolling through the Wyoming Dinosaur Center in Thermopolis. I've always been a fan of fossils, and find all that sort of thing fascinating. This museum also offered a ride out to their dig site along with the price of a ticket, but I was disappointed to find that it was too late in the day for the archeological tour. Too bad. I bought a ticket anyhow and strolled through their dioramas, wondering how much of it could have been reality. It was a nice little place, but I wanted to see bones coming out of the dirt, so I left just a little disappointed. There's that expectation thing rearing its ugly head again.

With a little investigation I found the Fountain of Youth Inn, right at the crossroads in Thermopolis, with a small diner in front of the motel. Gotta love it. The Fountain of Youth offered free access to a large hot spring in town, but it sounded like I'd have to get back on the bike to get there, so I skipped it. It felt good to just unpack and lay down.

I spent a good portion of that day following the Oregon Trail, thinking about Lewis and Clark and all the settlers that came after them. Once you're up into this part of the country, you can't avoid this kind of thinking; this is the beginning of white folks' history in this part of the country, and 150 years ago is not a whole lot of time. Poking around a web site later that night, I learned that around the turn of the 20th century, one of the more famous residents of Thermopolis was Butch Cassidy. How about that? With former residents like Cassidy, there wasn't much chance they were even going to notice me in that little town.

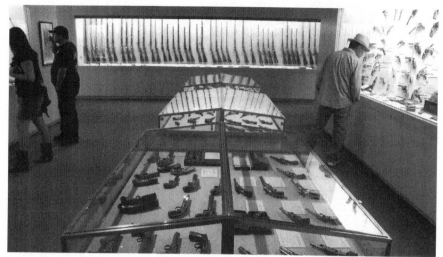

Cody Firearms Museum, Cody, Wyoming.

Mountain goats in Wyoming.

8/5/10 Thursday

It was a short ride this day, from Thermopolis to Cody, with a coffee break stop in Meeteetsee. Cody, Wyoming, is a town built around the memory of William Frederick "Buffalo Bill" Cody. He was an army scout and a buffalo hunter, but he made his name as a showman. His Wild West shows toured Europe and Great Britain as well as the U.S.A., and Buffalo Bill brought cowboys and Indians right into everybody's home town. William Cody actually helped to found the town that bears his name, in 1895. It is said that at the turn of the 20th century Buffalo Bill was the most well-known celebrity on earth.

I knew very little of this, of course, being a suburban punk from the Northeast. Once in Cody, I went to the Buffalo Bill Museum complex, which was fairly overwhelming. It's as if they dragged out every piece of history they could find in the state, and cart it up to Cody. The firearm museum was the most recommended attraction, prior to my arrival, and it is most impressive. It makes you want to run out right away and buy some guns. More guns, I mean!

Instead I went into the Sierra Trading Post determined to buy another knife, which I did. I got to talking with a very cute salesgirl there, who insisted that if I'm there on a motorcycle I had to meet her father. I was thinking maybe this was a little too soon, but it turned out her dad, another motorcycle enthusiast, also worked there; and she dragged him out to give me some local knowledge. I was wondering about riding a bike in Yellowstone, and he turned me on to a loop northeast of Yellowstone--Cody to Red Lodge, MT, to the Beartooth Highway over the pass to the Chief Joseph Scenic Byway, and back to Cody. About 170 miles of mind-blowing riding, he said.

It didn't take him long to convince me. Once I'd made the decision to take this ride, I found a cheap motel room and ditched all the bags except the tank bag, so I was on a small, light bike again, and it felt great. I figured I'd run up north, baggage free, not a care in the world, and ride the loop. Then I'd stay in Cody, and plan to hit Yellowstone fairly early in the morning.

The ride up to Red Lodge wasn't anything exciting, but it was empty and relaxing. The sun was bright on the road, as I headed north. The weather, for a change, was outrageously good; it looked like we were going to have a break in the thunderstorm schedule. Wide open blue sky, puffy clouds, just the right temperature for riding, and warm sun. Route 120 follows a wide valley north, hints of mountains to the west and falling off into hilly prairie to the east.

Of course, what I call prairie isn't really that. Every square inch of reasonably flat land in these parts is either plowed or fenced for livestock, so the "prairie" I've been talking about is either covered with grain, tilled and waiting for the next crop, or spotted here and there with cattle. If there is a real piece of prairie, it too has a fence around it, and a sign proclaiming what it is. Maybe the woman back at the hotel in Grand Forks wasn't far off the mark anyhow. She probably never has seen a prairie. I probably haven't either. But I have a good imagination.

It was 64 miles of good, clean asphalt up Route 120 and MT Route 308 to Red Lodge, and once there it was as simple as taking a left turn to get on the Beartooth Highway. There aren't a lot of roads to choose from here. Red Lodge looks like a fine little town to explore some day, chock full of bars and cafes and touristy attractions. But not this day; it was late afternoon and I was losing light.

The Beartooth follows another river valley for a ways before it starts climbing into the mountains, but from the outside edge of Red Lodge it's spectacular, and it only gets better as you climb. There's been plenty written about this road, and there's not much I can add to make it sound any better. Perfectly clean asphalt from edge to edge. Not a straight section to mar the ride, either rolling from side to side or deliciously curvy, climbing all the while on the way up from Red Lodge. At every turn the scenery gets more spectacular, and the best part? It was early evening and I was practically alone. No motorhomes, very few cars, a few other bikers, and no Johnny Law. There were other bikers in attendance though, most coming from the opposite direction and all returning the usual "biker wave" with a big grin.

At the top you arrive at Beartooth Pass, a plateau offering a view of jagged summits in every direction. The clouds were low and hiding the peaks of the western mountains in fog, and ragged bits of snowfields still painted the shady spots on the pass. A small herd of Rocky Mountain goats grazed around like a group of white-robed bearded wizards, and I just had to stop and check it out.

The animals weren't much afraid of anybody. It was fairly plain that they saw a lot of tourists, and had decided a while back that humans didn't pose much of a threat. That is, until a fellow biker decided to walk real close and point a video camera at them. Two of the goats started squaring off against each other, jousting as if on cue, bouncing on their hind legs and acting like they were about to fight. The few people watching thought it was cute. I got the impression that they were trying to spell out what might happen to any clown with a video camera if they took a mind to. Rocky Mountain goats are just big enough that you really wouldn't want to tangle with them. The two sparring goats edged closer and closer to the cameraman, who finally decided that easing back towards his Harley would be a good idea.

It was 50 miles of spectacular riding from Red Lodge to Chief Joseph Scenic Byway, easing through the late afternoon sunshine seven or eight thousand miles from home. Once again, I was right where I wanted to be; I could hear that bell ringing again. The road wasn't all perfect, there was a little bit of repaving going on beyond the Pass, and not without its micro-tragedy. At one point I was waved slow by a forest service person, and putted my way past a fancy SUV off in the ditch, right at a particularly pretty vista. It looked like the driver had one of those "Wow, look at that!" moments. The car looked like it went off the curve at a walking pace, and fetched up against a rock wall. I couldn't even see any damage.

The Chief Joseph Scenic Byway had a different feel, but was equally as impressive. The difference is that Chief Joseph is a more open road, cutting through canyons rather than following a ridge.

You can easily maintain a higher speed on it. Once again there was no automobile traffic, and now I had the lowering sun right behind me, lighting up the hills like they were painted with gold. What a great afternoon.

Half way down the Chief Joseph I passed an EMT vehicle screaming up from the opposite direction. If he was headed for the "wreck" on the Beartooth—and I couldn't imagine him racing towards anything else—it was quite a waste. And not very timely. A quick calculation put the scene of the crime a good 50 miles up the road behind me, and for a red and white box truck it was easily an hour's drive yet, and I had passed the accident 45 minutes earlier, at least. Wow. I remember when I was younger, we would have pushed that rig back onto the road, plugged up any bloody noses and gotten the heck out of there. Come to think of it, I would definitely still do the same today.

Thirty-six miles from the start of Chief Joseph, the road found its conclusion at Route 120, and I turned right to head back to Cody. That was the best riding of the trip, so far.

I zipped back to town and had some mediocre Mexican food in a restaurant full of tourists, then rode back to the motel in the fading light. Since all the luggage was off the bike, I took a little time in re-distributing the contents. I had already given Lucy everything that had remained unused since the beginning of the trip, including extra riding gear that I knew I wasn't going to wear. In the rain or the blazing heat, the most comfortable gear turned out to be the Aerostich Gore-Tex, and that's all I was going to wear the rest of the ride. My luggage was a lot lighter, and for the first time I was starting to feel organized. And, I had a new pocket knife to remember the Beartooth ride. I went to bed anticipating an early assault on Yellowstone in the morning.

Beartooth Highway, Montana.

8/6/10 Friday

I got up and out somewhat early this day, anticipating a fair number of tourists in Yellowstone and hoping to avoid them. Trouble was, there were a fair number of tourists with the same idea. It wasn't so bad going into the park from the Cody side, but once on the main park loop the traffic seemed to increase every minute. Of course, what this means is stop and go riding of monumental proportions.

Yes, there are plenty of natural wonders to see in Yellowstone, and since I'd never been there before I felt like I had to see it. But, we were in one section of the park, crawling along, and a small car full of Japanese tourists stopped in front of me to take pictures of a buffalo walking by on the side of the road. "Side of the road" means about eight feet away, and a full-grown American bison makes a

650 V-Strom look mighty small. Such a huge, matted, hairy beast, huffing by with just a hint of drool slobbering down his dirty chin (the bison, not me); it was as big as a Volkswagen Beetle. I was sitting there idling, trapped behind this rental Toyota feeling smaller and smaller as this gigantic bastard turned his wet, black, malevolent eye upon me, and I flashed on an image of me with innumerable broken bones and a wad of blue tin foil that used to be a fairly nice bike.

I started getting a little impatient after that—I have that tendency, occasionally. Okay. So the object of this little tour through the park was obvious, wasn't it? And this risking your life for tourism shit was getting old. I determined to work my way towards Old Faithful—why else would anyone go to Yellowstone?--and then once that obligation was filled I could escape from this beloved National Park with a clear conscience.

It was a terrible slog getting there. There are a certain class of tourists that should not be allowed to own cars. They drive at half the speed limit anywhere twisty or touristy—and I mean 15 mph in a 30—and then speed up to 60 mph in the passing zones, while the passing zone speed is only 45. Call me hard to get along with, but I find this particularly galling. I had to risk my life getting around people who, yes, did slow back down to 15 after the passing zone, holding up hundreds of other drivers who would be happy to just go the 30 mph speed limit.

Oh, and of course they'll stop in the middle of the road if there's any kind of critter alongside the highway. All I can say is, we're a very tolerant society. I've driven and ridden a lot in Europe, and in the old country drivers like that would be forced off the road and executed.

Old Faithful was a curious scene. I watched it do its thing with about two or three thousand other folks, and it is so consistent in its action I got to wondering if somebody's run a large pipe into the orifice just to make sure it kept going. Certainly, if it ever stopped I'd be surprised if the Park Service didn't do that, since all those folks standing around staring at the spray represent a whole pile of money to the park. Old Faithful is surrounded by massive parking lots, and a large overpass approach just to try to keep the traffic moving. Rather than a park full of natural wonders, Yellowstone was like trying to get through a very crowded mall parking lot when the carnival is in town. I wouldn't recommend it as a good thing to do on a bike, unless you're there well before or after typical vacation time. I'll bet you it's a lot nicer in late September.

I turned around and escaped out the south entrance, back onto Route 287. My plan was to head south on 287, then hook through the Grand Teton Park to Jackson, and then dip into Idaho before heading back north into Montana again. It wasn't a bad ride, after I passed a couple malingerers in motorhomes who were still basking in the glow of Yellowstone.

The Tetons are kind of indescribable. Yellowstone's surrounding country is hilly, and somewhat mountainous, but on the edge of a plain. As you ride south of West Thumb on the highway (287), the rolling hills of Yellowstone flatten out, but then all of a sudden these jagged mountains appear ahead and to the right. But it's not a huge range of mountains, like the Rockies. The Tetons are all packed in one spot, and they appear as if they were torn out of the ground by violent force, which is probably very true.

The highest mountain, Grand Teton itself, stands at 13,770 feet, which is definitely high enough to give you a headache. You get a sense of the overall height of the tallest mountains in the Tetons, but the real mindblower is their sheer, barren steepness. The Tetons are all rock, no green makes it into your view, just bare rock pointed straight to the sky.

Very impressive...but.... I would have dearly loved to linger and take it all in, but it was getting to be thunderstorm time once again. West and north of my position the sky was black and dense, and right where I was there was basically no shelter. My plan was to turn west at Jackson and around the other side of the Grand Tetons, and north through a bit of Idaho before crossing back into Montana again. There really wasn't anywhere else to go; I didn't want to run east or south, doing that would just move me backwards on the gameboard. It looked like I was going to get hit. I just hoped it wasn't a bad one.

Wrong again. The black clouds rushed down the valley like those videos of the pyroclastic flow off of Mount St. Helens, and swamped me in blinding rain and hail before I even had a second chance to suss out an escape route. Getting caught in a hailstorm in a car is a noisy, possibly damaging event. Getting caught in one on a bike is like all of a sudden having marbles sprinkled on you from about a half-mile up.

Now, the jacket has padded shoulders, that's okay. And if you have any sense you're already wearing a helmet, so that's not bad either. But those marbles find every other soft spot, like your arms and legs, the place on your back just behind the helmet, and the backs of your hands, and they start pounding those spots, leaving little black and blue bruises. At the same time, the cold rain and hail smear over the front of your face shield while the cold fogs the inside, and your visibility drops to about ten percent. To make matters worse on this day, all the car drivers started acting errati-cally—some stopped in the middle of the road, some jammed it into a lower gear and floored it--and I could smell my approaching death by motor vehicle. Time for an end-run.

I picked the first established road to the east and jumped onto it. It was a narrow paved road, coming from some ball fields, and even it was peppered with cars full of little leaguers and drivers not looking where they were going. I flipped up the face shield so I could at least see, introducing the hail now to the lower part of my face. Another hard gravel road offered a more northerly route, and I turned onto it and got on the gas.

It's hard for me to get the point across about how quickly and sometimes violently these storms come up; and then how quickly and violently I might react to it. Normally I'm just poking along, running with traffic if there is any, or running a few miles faster than the speed limit, but basically I blend in. When a storm rears up I turn into manic dirt biker trying to get away—from the other cars, as well as the weather. On this afternoon, I was spanking that

V-Strom down this unnamed gravel road, pointing it towards the only clear spot on the horizon. I jumped from one road to another, always aiming for clear sky, and finally came out of the storm, but God knows where.

I wasn't in the clear, because I still had to go north, where the storm was coming from. A few more twists and turns and I wound up in a little hamlet I later learned was called Kelly, "On the Gros Ventre." One building housed a coffee shop and snack bar, and a small shed across the way comprised the post office.

I quickly stopped, parked, and popped the seat off so I could stow the sheepskin pad in the topbox. When I had everything ship-shape I dashed into the coffee shop to wait out my second visit with the thunderstorm. Coffee sounded good, but there was a small cooler with beer in it, and a beer sounded better. By the time I picked one out and paid for it, the store was blasted with strong wind and hail, rain and big lightning. I shed my jacket and was content to be inside. If only they had a nice, soft easy chair!

I got to talking with a nice older couple, the Rileys, who happened to have kin in Keene, New Hampshire; Surry, actually. Did I mention before just how many people I was meeting who had friends or relatives in the Keene area? Not bad for a town of only 23,000 people. The Riley's and I talked about Wyoming and New Hampshire, and had a fine time for 20 minutes or so. I gave them my card, told them to contact me if they ever got back to Keene, and we'd have coffee at Brubakers.

When the weather broke I wiped the bike off and put the seat pad back on. Does it sound like I jealously guarded the welfare of my sheepskin pad? You betcha. I can't imagine squelching down onto that thing if it was soaked with rain and ice, and it had been taking care of my behind every day on this trip. It was only right that I should do my best to treat it well.

With the help of the GPS, I found my way back to the main road and into Jackson. It looked like a real cool town, ski town full of bars and restaurants. I stopped and made a few calls and figured out there was no way I could afford to stay in Jackson. I continued up into Idaho, and checked the GPS for rooms again, but a local rodeo had taken all the hotel rooms in some of the surrounding towns on my way, so I decided to head up to Route 20 and find a highway hotel.

And of course, this day was going to be a little different. I thought I had skirted around the only thunderstorms scheduled for that day, but now there was another one—north and west of me, of course, and headed my way. I had to make a decision—Route 33 and race right into it, hoping to find a place before it hit, or Route 32 and hope to run ahead of it and find something. I chose 32 and put my head down.

It was ominous. I was staying ahead of the storm, but just barely. Then, as I started getting closer to Route 20 the traffic picked up, all those good 'ol boys just like we've got in New Hampshire, 15 mph under the speed limit and no place in particular to go. I passed and raced and pissed people off, I'm sure, but got to Route 20 with smeary black storm clouds just rubbing on my back.

No time to think. I raced north on 20 about eight miles, just far enough to give myself some breathing room, and then sped off the highway into the parking lot of the first motel I saw. Got a room in record time, yanked off the one pannier bag I needed and jumped into the room just as the storm hit. I had pulled the bike right up onto the covered walkway in front of the door to the room. Fifteen minutes later all was calm, but the parking lot of the motel was running with two inches of water and pieces of broken-off tree limbs. Another narrow escape!

Of all the fine turn of events, this motel had a nice Mexican restaurant sharing the parking lot. Is it starting to become obvious what my favorite food is? I one time had a companion tell me, "I don't want to eat Mexican tonight, I had that last night." I pointed out to him if he was in Mexico, he'd be eating Mexican food every night. Which I could do. I could eat Mexican food three meals a day. I could live in Mexico, as a matter of fact, if I wasn't so rosy white and it wasn't so obvious I didn't belong there. I do enjoy the country and love the people, though. It makes me sad to hear about all the trouble they're having down there these days.

When the time came, I went across the parking lot and got a fine margarita and a chicken dinner. The chicken was cooked exactly the same as I'd had it at Terco's Pollito in Santa Rosalia, Baja, last time I was down there, and it was great. My only difficulty was I eventually became totally invisible to the young waitress and couldn't get a second drink. Couldn't get a check, from her, nothing. Such are the perils of traveling as a Party of One.

Grand Tetons and bison, Jackson, WY.

8/7/10 Saturday

The next morning I started early, and rode out of Ashton, ID, by about 9:00, and took Route 20 up to 87, then 287 all the way up to Browning, Montana. The ride I had planned was 405 miles, and I wanted to see how close I could come to the GPS' claim that it would take 6:08 to get there. I rode the first 300 miles non-stop, except for a pause for gas, and then had to break for lunch in Choteau. Nice little restaurant, but it cost me an hour. Then I forgot to fill up on the way out of town, and the next opportunity, 40 miles down the road, was 17 miles east. So I added a needless 34 mile round trip, just to tank up. Should be a lesson there.

But the riding was fantastic. Not high mountains, like the last few days, just hilly plains with high speed running the whole way. Speed limit of 70, top speed for the day was around 85-90. Beautiful roads. Great scenery--low green hills with a variety of flowers and different colored grasses. The temperature was cool enough to demand a T-shirt as well as a long sleeve T-shirt, plus the hand-grip heaters on at times in the morning. Misty air, the temperature close to the dew point, but no sign of rain all day, though clouds at times made it a little chilly. All in all, it was a long day but a great day of riding.

This trip through Montana completed the second goal of the trip. Montana was the last of the Lower 48 states that I hadn't been to, and now I can confidently claim that I've only got Alaska and Hawaii left on the roster of U.S. states I haven't visited. This was my first time to North and South Dakota, Nebraska, Wyoming and Montana, and I have to say I enjoyed them all. The plains of the first three might be flat and somewhat featureless, but there's such a sense of space there. Lots of open room, something we have precious little of on the East Coast. Wyoming was neat, in spite of Yellowstone and the tourists, and Montana is Big Sky country, as I was finding out. All very nice, and I hope to come back some day.

I stopped that evening at Jacobson's Cabins in East Glacier, Montana, a real nice place. I finally had a little "Unabomber" cabin to myself in Montana. I prefer cabin living to the average motel. I always liked it if we stayed in cabins on family vacations as a kid. Cabins, funky mom and pop motels, and lots of neon in the signs. That's what I like. And Mexican food.

I had a pretty good dinner at the counter in a cool little hippy restaurant in East Glacier, then walked down and self-toured the grand hotel down the road, the Glacier Park Lodge. The Great Northern Railroad built the Glacier Park Lodge in 1913, right after the railway depot was established. Glacier National Park was promoted as an easy destination from Chicago. Folks only had to get on the train and they'd be comfortably carried to the wilderness. It is a beautiful, impressive building, like most of the grand hotels from way back when. I was also pleased to see that the train station was active. Noting the V-Strom's title once again in my computer case, I could easily see getting on that train and heading to Chicago, and eventually the Amtrak Vermonter to within 20 miles of home. If need be. But I had plenty of riding I wanted to do before that would come about.

Old Faithful, and a few of my fellow humans.

Glacier Park Lodge, East Glacier, Montana.

8/8/10 Sunday

Got up early and headed north to the gates of Glacier Park. As soon as I left the cabin I could see the storm clouds brewing. The first part of the ride into Glacier was okay, but always with the threat of rain, and an occasional sprinkle. Going from east to west, the park is impressive. Violent mountain peaks and a ribbon of a road to ride on, hanging on the edge of swift destruction. Saw a few small glaciers, but then the rain started setting in. The second half of the road wasn't as interesting as the first half, and the exit from the park, on the west side, was the start of a giant traffic mess. Lots of cars and tourists, all with that Sunday afternoon get-the-last-bit-of-fun-in panic. People driving without looking, people wanting to go 80 mph, people who think Montana has no speed limit, and plenty of people who want to do 35 in a 70 mph zone.

I wound up tucking in and riding 80 miles across Montana without a break, and then finally stopping for lunch in Libby. No stop for water, no stop to pee, nothing. All on Route 2, and it's a crap road in this section. I finally got to Bonners Ferry, Idaho, and gave up for the night. In the future I hope to try not to schedule any serious travel for a Sunday afternoon in tourist country.

Still reeling from the forced march across the state, I met a fascinating guy at the hotel riding a Honda Gold Wing. We got into a conversation and wound up grabbing dinner together.

We soldiered our way through two great points of discussion: One, build a hydrogen/oxygen cracker into a typical motorcycle body, so that the bike can run on water. Easily done, since you can separate oxygen and hydrogen from water, and upon combustion the main byproduct is water vapor and water, which you can plumb back into the tank and crack again. A fairly small loss of liquid water could be replenished with the addition of distilled water from time to time.

Secondly was the notion that the story that oil is just recycled dinosaurs is a myth. Easy to refute, when you think long and hard about where the dinosaurs stand in the fossil record. From driving through the Dakotas and visiting the dinosaur museums, we know that the dinosaur fossil layer is right up near the top strata of rock (Mesozoic era). If all the dinosaur bones are high up in Mesozoic rock, why is all the oil 8000 feet below the surface? The oil didn't "trickle down" there. Look at the pressure exerted from the blown well BP drilled a mile below the Gulf. Figure out what sort of sea water pressure is on the well head, and look at the videos of the oil and gas gushing out of that broken well 5000 feet below. Oil, which is lighter than water, can't work its way down with all that pressure wanting to push it back up. Besides, there are no fossils down there. So where does the idea come from that rotted dinosaurs created oil?

My dinner partner claimed that oil is a renewable resource, that it is being generated constantly below the surface, as some kind of chemical reaction closer to the high-carbon interior of the planet. Interesting food for thought. Good oil geologists know this, he claims, but the myth is perpetuated to justify high prices and profits from petrochemical consumption. The price of gasoline can always be ratcheted higher when everybody believes we're running out of it.

He was also saying he had thought long and hard about working on a hydrogen generator as a car/bike fuel source, but he didn't want to be responsible for the loss of income for all the people directly affected by gasoline and oil sales. Also, one other guy who reportedly perfected a hydrogen cracker that used sound waves died mysteriously from food poisoning. Possibly he doesn't want that to happen to him. I said it would be fun to build a water-powered hydrogen bike and just keep it for your own use. Guaranteed no one would notice anything weird about it, people just don't pay that close attention to anything any more.

Since the trip I looked into the use of Brown's gas for fuel, which is the more or less official name for the "HHO" gas you get when you crack it out of water with electrolysis (HHO=two molecules of Hydrogen, one molecule of Oxygen). There are plenty of people selling systems to add onto automobile engines to supplement the use of gasoline, but precious little truly scientific research saying that it actually helps reduce gasoline consumption in a typical vehicle. Since then I've come to the conclusion that you could probably build a system large enough to create enough Brown's gas to run an engine, but I wonder if it would actually fit on a motorcycle. But, it was a very interesting topic of dinner conversation that night in Idaho.

Approaching Glacier National Park, Montana.

8/9/10 Monday

In the morning, I left Bonners Ferry on Route 2, and followed the Pend Oreille River for what seemed a long time before breakfast. Finally stopped at a little place in Priest River, with a waitress that was cute, blond, friendly, and my age range. She could have been 45, very upbeat and attractive. She seemed very out of control busy, so I offered to fill in as cook for her. There was some joking back and forth about it, but I wound up staying out of the kitchen. Little did she know that I really would have stayed and worked in the kitchen. It was barely ten o'clock, and I was already tired of riding.

It made an interesting daydream, as I rolled down the road with my belly full. That American dream of wandering off to God-knows-where, pull into a luncheonette and wind up slinging hash for not much more than minimum wage, while your new found potential girlfriend fixes up a junky old one room apartment above her garage, that hasn't been used since she moved in three years ago with her biker old man, who's doing three to five for some sort of unexplained mischief. I'm sure Tom Waits has sung a song like that. It'd be all right; be an interesting gig until the road started calling again.

While I was in the diner, I noticed there was another biker couple inside, sitting at a table across the room. Then, when I was about done, another lone adventure-bike rider came in, kinda rough looking, wearing Gore-Tex, carrying a helmet. I talked to him. He was out on a KLR, just his second or third day out; trying to stick to camping, but already in need of a square meal.

Adventure riders are a different breed. Loners. I see Harley guys always in twos or more--twos, threes, or six or seven at a time. Gold Wing guys are sometimes alone, but normally in pairs. But adventure riders are usually alone. Sometimes I see them in groups, two or three riders, but rarely. I talked to the KLR guy for a few minutes, and he seemed grateful for the acknowledgement. I had a vision of a diner with five or six adventure riders in it, all at separate tables, all facing away from each other. All with Gore-Tex jackets hanging over the opposite empty seat or draped across it, and with helmets on the table. It would make a funny cartoon.

Route 2 out of Idaho was not very interesting, but as soon as Washington got under the front wheel everything looked better. I turned north on Route 20 at Newport and all the traffic went south on Route 2 toward Spokane. Wonderful. Even better, the GPS had picked out a back road from Usk to Chewelah that turned out to be a perfect diversion. Fast, smooth and covered with tasty curves. And, the road was so clean it was almost as if it had been power-washed just for me. Oddly, all the roads in Washington would turn out to be just as clean.

I turned north on Route 395 on the other side of the Chewelah road, and then back up to 20 again. The roads were excellent and the scenery even better. My friend in Idaho had told me about

Route 21 south from 20, and suggested I take it. So, when it came up on the left, that's the way I turned.

And I'm glad I did; it turned out to be one of the highlights of the trip. 53 miles long, limited access from the sides (dirt roads coming into it) and at the bottom a ferry waited to take you across the Columbia. Pretty scenery, just pastures and small farms top to bottom, walled in by rock canyon walls barely more than a quarter mile apart the whole way. Way too much fun.

Near the bottom of this section of 21, a side road goes off west towards the Grand Coulee Dam, but I had to take the ferry. Maybe it held 12 cars, at most. There were three on this day, and three bikes. The crossing only took ten minutes, and it was free. On the other side, Route 21 continued for another curvy 14 miles, and then ended at the town of Wilbur. Route 174 west heads to the dam, which I had to see, of course, so there I went.

All of the roads after the crossing of the Columbia were bounded by endless wheat fields, just golden grain as far as you could see. Late in the season like this, in the late afternoon light, everything was a ripe gold color. Rolling yellow hills and black roads winding in and out. Just fantastic.

Grand Coulee has a big dam, three small towns, and I fortunately found a cheap motel with a laundry room, because I had no clean clothes. The room had a bed with a thick memory foam pad on it, and it was great. Had it been located in an attractive place, I may have stayed an extra day, just to catch some rest. But it was on a dusty street overlooking a dusty town, a town that was obviously built quickly to serve the workers building this dam years ago. The place didn't have much to offer, so I moved on.

Waiting for the ferry. Lake Roosevelt, Columbia River, Washington.

8/10/10 Tuesday

Took 155 out of Grand Coulee, back up to Route 20. Back into Indian country, the Colville Indian Reservation. Route 20 didn't disappoint again, with not too much traffic and lots of sweeping curves. Suddenly the road dropped me into the cowboy town of Winthrop, and that quick I went from Indian country to tourist country. Winthrop was one of those towns settled quickly in the late 1800s when gold fever struck the west. When the gold stopped panning out, the town just idled along, secluded in the Washington back country, but then when Route 20 came through in the late 1970s the town government got the idea for a full Western makeover. The end result is some kind of a cross between Deadwood and Disney. It's neat-looking from the street, but up close it's souvenirs and ice cream shops; fine if you like that sort of thing, but I stayed on the highway.

After Winthrop the scenery just got better and better. I was climbing into the North Cascades, and I will defy anyone to come up with country that is more rugged, or more mouth-dropping scenic. The road climbed up to Washington Pass, at 5477 feet, then Rainy Pass at 4855. Even though this area is so much lower than the Rockies in Colorado, there is still snow at altitude and the air is cold.

After Winthrop I had stopped to put on a sweatshirt, waterproof gloves, and tape up the vents in my boots, because of an approaching storm. I wasn't too happy about it, but what the hell. I started riding again and realized I'd left my wallet in my back pocket. Stopped, opened the jacket and put the wallet inside, where it's waterproof, and then try to fumble the neck closed again, not getting it nearly as good this time. But I was right in time for the rain, which lasted all of a quarter-mile. Then it was done. Typical daily weather.

But the air kept getting colder, and damper. The clouds boiled around the summits at Washington Pass, and when I came back down the other side it only got warmer for a few minutes, it seemed. Then it just kept getting colder, and damper. I realized this was because I was finally on the other side of the Cascades, and this was my fist taste of the Pacific coast climate. It would be with me, on and off, for a good while; all the way to San Francisco.

I got down the hill and into Sedro Woolley. I was spent, but remembering the other recommendations Dick gave me, I decided to take the loop up to Mt. Baker. The only way there was Route 9 to 542. The total round trip was about 135 miles, but it was worth it. The road goes all the way to the top of Baker, where you can see a glacier, and plenty of last winter's snow still trying to melt. The road up Baker is epic, a real footpeg dragger.

At one point on the way up, a rider went by me on a roadrace bike with a tag wired onto it. The rider--a woman, as it turned out—came by a little too close and about 6000 rpm higher in the rev range than necessary, and just about scared me out of the seat. She was followed quickly by a guy on a Husky 630 motard bike, who looked like he was enjoying staying right on her tail. When I got to the top I rolled over to talk to the Husky guy, and it turned out that he was riding with this woman on the track bike, who was big, wrapped in black leather and without a doubt the most macho person on the summit that day. But, she was also pissing and moaning about how he shouldn't have passed her back there, that she was supposed to be leading so that meant he should stay behind her... and it went on and on, with no sign of her grumpiness abating. It made me glad, once again, that I was riding solo for this trip.

I rode back down, through the village of Clipper, believe it or not, and found lodging in Sedro Woolley. I had high hopes for Clipper, but it was barely more than a bump in the road. At least, years back, when I drove through Hot Coffee, Mississippi, they had a sign welcoming you there. There wasn't much more than a couple tired-looking houses in Clipper. If it was really me, I'd give you a better welcome.

I called my friend Dorian in Olympia, who would be meeting me in the morning and hosting me for a couple of days. It would be an interesting ride down to Olympia. I would mark my arrival on the West Coast by following Route 20 out onto Whidbey Island and down to Oak Harbor, where I would once again get on a ferry, this time to begin riding south for the first time in the trip.

North Cascades, Washington.

8/11/10 Wednesday

Breakfast in the morning was as convenient as across the parking lot, to a pretty good diner next door. I even allowed myself to sleep late, if you consider 7:30 a late rising time. It was bound to be a fairly easy morning, since I only had to ride to the ferry at Oak Harbor, and then take a boat across the top of Puget Sound to Port Townsend.

I was dog-tired, but was starting to feel like I had accomplished something. I had still been violating the cardinal rule of cross-country riding, and not writing down my mileage; but as near as I could figure I had ridden about 7000 miles to get to this point. As I cruised through the winding roads on the way to Oak Harbor, I kept looking out for my first view of the sea. Soon enough, it was there, a glimpse of water between the trees, strip malls and vacation homes. Whidbey Island is pretty much flat, so I didn't get the triumphant hilltop view of the Pacific Ocean we always imagine, but I knew where I was. I was as far west as I was going to get, this trip. It felt good.

I arrived characteristically early for the ferry, and spent time chatting with other folks waiting for the boat. One was a gentleman slightly older than me, on a spotless BMW touring bike. He said he was a salesman, a traveling salesman I presumed, and said that a few years ago he decided his passion for riding wasn't taking enough of his leisure time, so he traded in his Cadillac for a BMW bike. Now he rode to all his meetings, and just loved every day. I got the impression that not everything he said was gospel, but that would be par for a salesman.

One thing I did notice was he was carrying a small stainless steel Thermos bottle, full of coffee. One of those, "Why didn't I think of that?" moments. I had two small vacuum bottles like that at home, and one should have been with me.

The boat arrived and we all rolled on. What a glorious thing, to be back on the water, on the other side of the country. It was a big boat, and a smooth ride, and the day was gorgeous, bright sunny weather. The cruise across took only about 40 minutes, and we were soon unloading—motorcycles first off, of course.

I pulled into a parking lot right off the ferry dock, and waited for Dorian. I had actually never met him before, but when he read in Trail Rider magazine that I might be planning a trip, he sent me a note and invited me to his home, and offered to show me around the region. I accepted immediately, of course, which should serve as a lesson to everyone else who might consider such a thing: be careful what you wish for!

When Dorian arrived we found a tragically hip little place for lunch, and sat down and got to know each other. Dorian's a big guy, with a serious expression that does a great job of covering up his inner child, which is still alive ad well. Short, slightly graying hair, moustache, and a simmering passion for all things involving two wheels and an engine. I could tell he was feeling me out, seeing what I was capable of on two wheels. That helped me relax—I could tell he had a no-nonsense attitude, and wasn't going to take me out and injure me right off.

Our first hour together went well. I can say with confidence that there were no surprises; and I'm sure he could say the same thing about me. If you've met one middle-aged dirt biker, you've met them all. We pretty much share all the same passions, one way or another, and our similarities make it easy to feel comfortable right away.

Port Townsend was a cool little town to visit, but we were soon on our way south to Olympia. Only another hundred miles, but it was getting warmer and I was getting more tired by the minute. By the time we arrived at Dorian and his wife Robin's cozy little house in Olympia, I had bags under my eyes that were hiding my double chin. Dorian was full of ideas of where we were going to ride and what we were going to see, but once he took a good look at me sans helmet, he said, "You're not riding anywhere tomorrow."

On the ferry to Port Townsend.

Dorian and the bikes in Port Townsend.

8/12/10-8/14/10

Bless you, my son. Instead we took the day and toured around the industrial areas of Seattle, with a stop at Touratech USA's headquarters, and to Dorian's local BMW shop, South Sound BMW. You see, Dorian owns a BMW GS1150, and from the moment I landed he tried hard to get me to trade in my Suzuki on a Beemer, so I could ride back in real comfort. He made a compelling argument—mostly based on his opinion that BMWs were just plain better—but I stayed on the little Suzuki.

I spent the next three days with Dorian and Robin, and though I did manage to stay off the bike that Thursday (August 12), on Friday we were back in the saddle. We talked about a lot of ambitious ideas, and in the end we decided to make it a fairly long day and take a loop around both Mt. Saint Helens and Mt. Rainier.

So we got out early and headed east, sun in our faces and blazing heat even at nine o'clock in the morning. It was just my luck that I had apparently dragged a heat wave along with me, and the legendary rainy suburbs of Seattle were breaking temperature records. I have said that I don't like riding in heat, right? At least in the northwest it was slightly lower humidity that what I'd started with in Vermont. Not a whole lot lower. But we rode through some beautiful farm country, and worked our way up into the foothills of the Cascades.

It was eerie to sit at the lookout and actually see St. Helens up close. We stopped at all the spots that recorded the big eruption 20 years ago, and finally took a break at the lookout at Windy Ridge. The most alarming thing about St. Helens is that it is still alive. Sitting at Windy Ridge and watching the huge crater left by the explosion 20 years ago, you can see that rocks are still tumbling and the ground is still steaming in spots. Looking to the north at Spirit Lake, it's also surprising to see that the surface of the water is still covered with logs; what used to be huge evergreens, blown down by the explosion. The overall impression was one of impending cataclysm, like looking at a box of dynamite bouncing around on the tailgate of a moving pickup truck. It didn't take long before we were ready to move to safer ground.

Safer ground--like Mount Rainier? Rainier is a regal mountain, a snow capped cone that pops up and takes your breath away, no matter where you are in the Seattle area. You'll be driving along, not even thinking about it, and suddenly there it is, right in front of you. It is massive. Every time I saw it, it gave me the chills.

And Rainier is not a comforting presence. If Rainier some day goes the same way as St. Helens, depending on the direction it decides to blow, it could ruin life for millions of people in the Seattle/ Tacoma region. I thought it felt a little like sharing space with a time bomb. But, at the same time, it's a very impressive sight when you're out cruising around on a bike.

Our loop finished up as a 300 mile day, in 90 degree-plus heat. By the time we got back to the Olympia suburbs we were ready for a few cold beers. I did notice at that point that the trip odometer was showing 7900 miles.

We had spent a little bit of time on Thursday afternoon fitting tires, Continental TKC80s I had shipped there previously. They were a little improvement over the smooth tires, especially for the gravel roads, so we rode west on Saturday for a quick 130 mile loop on the dirt roads of the Olympic Peninsula. There is so much to explore in that part of the world that I decided right then and there that I would have to move to Washington just to learn it all. And one day, it just might happen.

Dorian and Ranier.

8/15/10 Sunday

By Sunday I figured my hosts were entitled to at least one weekend day together, so I packed up my bags and prepared to head out again. Dorian and Robin had been great hosts, and I promised them I'd be back; if not to visit, to live there. I understand that this region sees an inordinate amount of rain in most seasons, but this was the second or third time I'd been to Washington when the weather was clear and sunny, and I'm starting to get the idea that maybe the myth—that western Washington is all about rain—doesn't quite jive with the reality. Like I said, I might have to move there and check it out.

I left Olympia early in the morning, getting out before the heat started building, and stopped an hour later at an AHRMA vintage motocross race at Chehalis. I wondered if I could get through it incognito, but one guy recognized me, and I'm sure we'd met at one of the ISDT Reunion Rides in the past. It was fun to watch a few motos full of old, old bikes, but one particularly ugly-looking pile-up on the start straight brought back the reality of motorcycle racing. Everybody eventually walked away from it, but man, we're talking a lot of old guys on old, ill-handling bikes with no suspension. Crashing is not the thing you want to be doing on a vintage bike.

Long about 11:00 it started getting seriously hot, so I left there and headed west to the coast, hoping for a more moderate temperature and getting my wish. It started cooling down after 45 miles, when the road, Route 6, started working its way through the coastal hills. By the time I reached the coast road, Route 101, at about 75 miles, it was downright cold. I was happy to finally see the Pacific Ocean proper when I turned south at Willapa Bay.

It was early in the day, so I could see no real reason to stop for the night, though I was sorely pressed to just sit on the foggy beach and watch the waves, with Otis Redding going through my head. No, it wasn't San Francisco, but it was the Pacific, finally.

I found a sufficiently funky looking little diner in South Bend, built out of an old trolley car, by the looks of it. Another one of

The end of the trail for Lewis and Clark.

my travel preferences. Always eat local, and the weirder the place looks, the more fun it is. The food? Well, I have to say that I hadn't had anything much more than average food anywhere I stopped, but sometimes things taste magical when you're in a strange place, dog tired, or starving from being on the road all day. So it works out.

After lunch I decided to dawdle my way down the coast until I found a cool place to stay. I went to the Lewis and Clark Center at the National Park of the same name, just to pay my final respects. My ride had been crossing paths with those two ghosts since Minnesota, and it was finally time for us to go our separate ways. I had been reading the Lewis and Clarke journals since some point earlier in the trip when I picked the book up at another L&C tourist stop—there's a few of them out there. Lewis and Clarke were happy to see the Pacific too, but they arrived at a time when the weather was foul, and they were pinned down on the beach and denied even a glimpse of the ocean for weeks once they got there. I had none of those problems. I just bade adieu to Fort Clatsop, and headed south on my bike.

I hadn't counted on the coast of Oregon being a shore resort, but it is. There was lots of traffic going in and out of Astoria, but I ducked onto BR101 and took the L&C Highway into Seaside. Seaside was a zoo. I was there in the peak of vacation season, and people were partying as if it was their last weekend on Earth. There had to be some place quieter.

One interesting thing happened in Seaside, though. I wanted to see the beach, so I hunted for a side road that would take me there. I threaded my way through crowds of people walking blindly into traffic, girls in bikinis talking on cell phones, boys carrying boogie boards, moms pushing strollers with babies frying in the sun, it was mayhem. I finally scooted to the end of a street and there it was, salt water and sand. I shut the bike off and took a deep breath of the salt air, and looked around. Hey, I had been there before.

It slowly dawned on me that the last time I was in Oregon, I was here with Todd, a friend who worked for me at the magazine. We were killing time at a KTM dealer show in Portland, and decided to take the rental car out to the coast to see the Oregon ocean, something neither of us had seen before. We roared down to the coast road, made a right, made the first left, and walked out on the beach. And I had just walked out onto the same beach, from a way different direction. This was only the second time I had ever seen the sea coast of Oregon, and here I was in the same spot.

I had dawdled away enough time, so I started hunting for a room. Seaside was out of the question, no room anywhere. Went down the coast, checking the GPS as I rode, and finally found suitable lodging in Manzanita. More than I like to spend, $110, but beggars can't choose. It was the Sand Dune Inn, four blocks from the beach. The hotel owner was an ex-pat Brit named Brian, who

possessed that typically dry English sense of humor that is so refreshing when you're out on the open road. Brian said his task was
to "tend to the weary" there on the Oregon coast, and he does a
good job of it.

Every good motel has a neon sign.

8/16/10 Monday

Morning came around and it was nice and cool, damp and about 55 degrees. I walked down to the beach, got a cup of coffee and a donut on the way. Nice. People with dogs, one surfer gal in wetsuit who didn't know how to surf. Packed up and rode up to the local diner for breakfast, then hit the road.

There was about 20 minutes of good riding. Then it became obvious that the coastal traffic was going to be a problem, top to bottom. Traffic was bad. Every little town was a snarl of cars, for no reason that I could see. Why would you want to be driving around, when you were supposed to be relaxing at the beach for your vacation? Everyone stayed on 101, even if an alternate route existed. I followed the GPS around the outside of towns a couple of times, took the scenic route around, through the industrial parks and funky neighborhoods, all the while I was still moving instead of stopped. The stop and go got worse as I headed south. Finally, after about 100 miles of this abuse, I peeled off onto Route 20 and headed inland.

Lucy had suggested Crater Lake as an interesting sight, so I had already decided to visit there. Crater Lake was at least 100 miles south of where I turned away from the beach, and 100 miles inland, but I'd had enough of the stop and go and left the coast early.

Maybe it was a bad idea. As I crossed the Coast Range the heat increased. By the time I got to Corvallis the heat was stifling. Hard to even breathe. I stopped for fuel and ice cream, and made arrangements for a motel up the road in Steamboat, on the way to Crater Lake. I generally don't like to make reservations ahead, but sometimes you need a target to aim for. Plus, I was pretty sure this place was the only motel way up in this woody little town (and I was right). Of course I broke at least one rule, and didn't ask if there was a restaurant within walking distance. I hate having to get back on the bike after I get off it at night, and this night I had to drive 10 miles back down the hill for dinner. Had I known ahead of time, I would have eaten on the way. Got a good burger at a small joint in

Glide, OR, though.

I had to wait out the sun before dinner, though, once I arrived at the motel. I waited for it to drop behind the hill 'til I could go outside without broiling any more. The desk clerk told me the high there that day was an even 100 degrees. Not a good temperature for riding, I can tell you that.

It was a great road coming up from the freeway, though. When I hit the heat in Corvallis I had decided to take the bit in my teeth and high-tail it south as quick as I could go. That meant slabbing it on Route 5, which sucked. The good road came up from Wilbur to Glide, following the North Umpqua River. Nice, twisty, no guard rails, and exceedingly scenic. The road wound around through hills and cliff edges, always showing a gorgeous view of the river way down below. The motel guy said it was dangerous at night, I could see why. But it was a nice way to end a hot, tiring day.

On the road from Wilbur to Glide.

8/17/10 Tuesday

Got up early to beat the heat, got on the road at seven and the temperature was all right. Stopped at Toketee Falls to walk the trail and check it out—who can resist a waterfall? I parked next to a car with two dogs in the back seat. I was talking to them, until I realized someone was asleep in the front seat, a girl, I thought. I hiked up to check out the falls, then walked back to see that it was a girl, she was putting away her backpacking stove after making breakfast, I guess. I told her I'd already been greeted by her dogs, she said they were her car alarm.

I wound up finding breakfast at a lodge just outside of Crater Lake Park. It was still early, the weather was nice. I got up into the park and couldn't believe the scenery. What a pretty spot. Huge blue lake tucked into an equally huge volcanic crater. I couldn't take the boat tour since the next available was at 3:00, and I knew I didn't want to be there in the heat of the afternoon. Instead, I rode around the crater and checked it out.

By ten o'clock the sun was starting to burn my back. The crater rim sits at something like 6500 feet, so the air was still comfortable, but as I dropped down the south side it just got hotter and hotter. The weather forecast said it was only going up to 88 that day, but it felt a lot warmer than that. My destination was back to the coast and down into California, and I knew if I just got over the Coast Range again the temps would fall quickly.

Sure enough, 45 miles down the road from Medford (on Route 199) the air started to freshen, and in another 20 miles it was finally cool again. I was grateful to have the coastal weather to fall back on, but was starting to get concerned about working my way back east. Especially getting through the desert and going into Arizona. I was thinking I might have to ride at night just to stay reasonably cool. Or ride early in the morning and quit at noon. I'm not a big fan of sharing the road with critters in the dark, so I mused on this subject as I wound my way through the Siskiyou Mountains and down into California redwood country.

Crater Lake, Oregon.

I wanted to see some trees, so I stopped at the Redwoods ranger station for information. They pointed me towards a dirt road so I could ride through a redwood grove. It was a good tip, very awe-inspiring to ride through those trees, but it was incredibly dry and dusty. And of course choked with cars, some trying to go too fast and kicking up way too much dust, as assholes in cars will do. I turned around after about three miles, and went back onto 101. Then I learned that 101 goes right through an old-growth redwood forest anyhow.

I looked for a motel in Crescent City, a town with little or no visual appeal. But, they did have the Curly Redwood Lodge, so I stopped there. It was an attractive little place in the age-old motor court style, with a very woody difference. In 1952, lightning struck a giant redwood near the Crescent City airport. The tree had to be cut down, so a local entrepreneur bought it and had it sawn into planks, all 57,000 board-feet of it. From that wood, this motel was created. The Lodge opened in 1957, with all of the paneling, doors, trim and details milled from this one tree. It's a very cool place, with big rooms, and yes, there is a neon sign out front.

I had dinner at a local restaurant across the street. The food was forgettable, but the cooler case was full of outrageous looking desserts, and a banana cream pie caught my eye. I asked for a piece of it to go so I could have a midnight snack after tending to all my evening chores. I tucked into it late that night, and was horrified to find out the foolish waitress cut me a piece of coconut cream pie by mistake, which is not even a poor substitute. You know, I'm lactose intolerant, and I do not have a casual attitude towards cream pies (though I do take the pills with good results). To me, a good banana cream pie is bliss, and a coconut cream pie is an abomination. Words could not describe my disappointment, and even a year later I still get a twinge of regret from the experience.

At the Curly Redwood Lodge in Crescent City.

8/18/10 Wednesday

The ride started with a low ceiling and cold temperatures, and remained that way most of the day. I started out wearing a T-shirt and sweatshirt, and then added the electric vest later on--and needed it. The riding was beautiful. Much less traffic on the California coast than on the Oregon coast, and I would have never believed that. Northern California just isn't quite as developed as Oregon is.

I rode down through the redwood forests along 101, and was amazed at how many big redwood trees there are. Places where the road just snakes through the trees, no wider than two cars. Places where the trees arch up to cover the top of the road like a canopy. Beautiful stuff. Stopped for coffee and a sandwich at a small town called Benbow, and then kept moving south.

One thing I haven't mentioned is blackberries. Something about the western coastal climate encourages the growth of blackberry bushes, and I had been riding past them ever since I crossed the Columbia on the Washington and Oregon border. They are always alongside the road, and in places they grow in great profusion. I'd been stopping occasionally and eating them, and actually picked up a little poison ivy on my arms, because the ivy likes the climate too, I guess. I have a variety of berries growing on my land back home, and make preserves every year, so having an unlimited supply of free berries on hand just adds to the appeal of the northwestern coast. As I continued south in California the number of blackberry patches had been dwindling, and I was starting to see the end of my favorite roadside snack.

In Leggett I hit the start of California Route 1, and the fun began. The Pacific Coast Highway. The last time I had been on this section of road was 1973, 37 years ago, driving a rented AMC Gremlin, and I remember being greatly fatigued at the end of it. This time I had the right vehicle and I scuffed the tires big time all the way down to Fort Bragg. This top section of the Coast Highway is nirvana on a good motorcycle. It is largely empty of tourists, and only trafficked by local drivers who know they're struggling to get the car through all the twists and turns.

Most drivers were really courteous and got out of the way in the pull-outs. One "Just Married" car poked along and hogged the road, appearing scared to death in spite of California license plates. Must think since they're just married they have everything to live for, and have to be careful. I'm divorced--I don't give a shit. In the first 40 miles of that road I balled up the rubber on the tires and turned both brake rotors blue. And enjoyed every minute of it.

Complicating the ride is the scenery, which is gawdawful beautiful, even on a grey overcast day. I don't think the ocean ever disappoints, any ocean, but the California coast has to be the best. Many times I was torn between looking to the right at the scenery or staying focused on the road roaring by. I hit a nice balance, but like I said, my tires got a workout.

I had a late start in the morning getting organized, so it was a late finish at the end of the day. But I finished the ride in a good position to get to the Bay Area the next morning for lunch with Dr. Fred and a little tooth inspection. That was my next planned destination. Dr. Fred Cameron is a former ISDT rider, and a dentist in Corte Madera. I had been handed a suspicious bill of goods from a local dentist before I left home, and I wanted Fred to give me a second opinion.

So Point Arena looked to be a suitable place to spend the night, and I stayed at a motel there that would have been typical in Mexico. The parking lot was almost full, but close inspection revealed that most of the cars had been abandoned there. Most had flat tires, broken windows, etc. Junk was everywhere, and four ragged children played in the parking lot, two black and two white. The room was just as ragged, mis-matched patches of dirty carpeting, no window screens, little furniture, towels were a variety of colors. The bathroom was filthy, with a "Sanitized" ribbon across the toilet seat, Probably only because it's required in California. You don't have to clean the toilet, you only have to say you did.

Noise started in the parking lot as the night came on, mostly people banging things around and dogs growling and fighting. Just like Mexico, except the stray dogs in Mex are friendlier. Also, in Mexico the room would have been $25; here it was $60. Oddly, there was a great Italian restaurant up the street, where I found one of the best meals of the trip. Spaghetti Bolognese and a salad, garlic bread and a little wine. Oh, and it was also expensive. Welcome to California.

Riding through the land of the Redwoods.

California coast.

8/19/10 Thursday

Easy day today. I left the motel without breakfast, and rode to a small village farther down the coast, to a trendy coffee and tea shop. Nice place. Friendly, pretty woman working there, had little chance to talk after a local came in and they got to talking about boats. I can't figure the area out. Very nice houses on the beach side of Route 1, but nobody seems to be in them. Must be weekend houses for city folk. The locals all seem to be ranchers or construction workers, though there's not many of them. Must be all wealthy weekenders or retired folks who own all the property.

Route 1 was still a pleasure, but on this morning it was socked in with coastal fog. Below 180 feet altitude (on the GPS) I'm under the layer; anything above that and I'm socked in. It must be possible around here to be walking down the street with your head in the fog, and if you stoop down things will clear up. Head in the clouds, for sure.

It was somewhere along this coast, early this morning, when I finally had the feeling that I was a long, long way from home. Not feeling lonely, particularly, but definitely alone in the fog, trying to at least keep it up to 35 mph with everything a blinded gray, following the painted centerline—thank goodness it was there.

But, this was my first feeling that I had gone about as far as I could with this trip, definitely as far west as I could go. The ocean was beautiful, but I had a hankering for the desert, and I knew it was coming up next.

I came off of Route 1 outside of Bodega Bay, where I had a proper breakfast at the Tides Wharf Inn. The dining room sits on the water, where I watched sea lions swimming lazily in the bay and a small whale rolled by. Very nice, and I knew this was going to be my last taste of a peaceful California coast for a while.

After breakfast I ditched the foggy coast road and rode out to Route 101 to try my luck with city traffic. The traffic increased exponentially as I worked my way up to Dr. Fred's office. I found him easily enough, just in time for lunch. He checked my teeth out, and sure enough the local dentist (who was not my normal dentist) was trying to cheat me. Can you imagine someone willing to drill holes in sound teeth just to make money? Fred did find one tooth that was badly cracked (not on the local dentist's work order, by the way) and fitted me for a crown, which he would have the lab send to me farther down the road.

Fred was heading to New England, of all places, the next day; so we had to part ways and I worked out a room in San Francisco for the night, just for something different. On the way there, I jumped off 101 at the last exit north of the Golden Gate Bridge, and took the road to Point Bonita. If you pick your way up the hill here, you will find the classic tourist photo-op of the bridge, and I did just that, of course. Trouble was, the bridge was already socked in with the afternoon fog, and it was hard to get a good shot of the scene. I set the bike up in the right place, took up position and waited. People came and went, took their pictures and gawked at the bridge, and every now and then I got a chance to take a shot when the cloud cleared somewhat. At best, I got a picture of just the top of the bridge, but it's still instantly recognizable.

If you've never seen it, your life won't be complete until you see the fog rolling in over San Francisco, and this lookout over the Golden Gate Bridge is the best place to do it. The fog is a living thing there, and every afternoon it pushes its way back from its resting point out over the ocean. When the fog, which is incredibly dense, hits these coastal hills it piles up on the seaward side until it reaches the crest, then it pours over the hills like milk flowing over a pile of Cheerios. On the way down the hill, the fog fills up all the little hollows before spilling over once again, and on a very calm day it will wash over your feet and then slowly work its way higher. It is such a strange feeling to be waist-deep in a moving cloud, and San Francisco is the place you can see it happen.

My bargain motel in San Francisco was dirty, the wireless didn't work, checking in was an incredible 45 minute hassle, and the streets in the Tenderloin are full of hustlers, beggars, and bums

Golden Gate Bridge, San Francisco, California.

passed-out on the sidewalk. I had to step over a passed-out bum on the sidewalk to get back into my room, after a really good Thai dinner in a local restaurant—I was the only non-Thai person there, go figure. San Francisco was one of the few times I was genuinely concerned about the safety of the bike, so I unloaded all the baggage, attached all the locks to it and hoped for the best.

Point Arena Lighthouse, California.

8/20/10 Friday

After a lousy night's sleep, I rolled out way early to check and see if the bike was still there. I was happy to see it still chained to its parking spot, so I quickly loaded all the bags back on. I got out of the motel at 7:00, careful not to step on any sleeping homeless, and went for a ride around the city. Very neat place. Alarmingly hilly. Being early in the day there wasn't much traffic; everybody was probably still fighting their way out of the suburbs and across the bridges. That left me somewhat alone with the town, and if it wasn't for the traffic lights I would have played "Bullitt" on the V-Strom. Yeah, I still stop at traffic lights. Silly, isn't it?

I always thought that San Francisco would be a great town to explore with a partner, but I haven't got enough interest to want to do it alone. Early morning on a bike was fun, looking down the steep, steep hills they built these city streets on. I looped back across to the east, to the Embarcadero and saw the Bay Bridge, then rode all the way up past Fisherman's Wharf to the Presidio and hooked a left onto Route 1, where the traffic was quickly getting thicker. I rode through Daly City and Pacifica, then the road narrowed down again and started to get more fun.

Stopped in Pacifica for breakfast at a Denny's, because I didn't want to have too much fun on an empty stomach. I read the newspaper while I was there, and struggled internally with a problem I knew I was going to have to address. You see, I had been on the road for over a month, and all that time my hair was trying to grow inside of a helmet. I have thick hair that requires a lot of discipline in the best of circumstances. In the confined space of a helmet, the hair grew weirdly, and I was now starting to look like an albino Buckwheat. With the helmet off, no amount of soaking or combing could keep it pointed in any reasonable direction. Something had to be done, and since there was a giant strip mall behind the Denny's, I knew there had to be a Supercuts or something, and I was right. It was time to get a trim.

Have you ever walked into a place and immediately thought you were making a big mistake? It was not a Supercuts, it was a clone, and as soon as I walked in I was accosted by a woman who could have been the Wicked Witch from the Wizard of Oz. She had stringy black hair, with a bald spot, crooked teeth and a wart on her nose. Before I knew what was happening, she had thrown me into a chair and lashed me down with the toga they wrap around you. She started hacking at me with an electric trimmer, and when that didn't do what she wanted she starting tugging clumps of hair right out of my skull. The wildly buzzing machine slashed and whacked and stalled in the bigger clumps, and I stopped her when I couldn't stand the pain any more. She asked about my moustache, and then started grinding away at it, still with the dog trimmer. I left bruised and bloody, but at least my hair was shorter. I wasn't aware of the real damage she'd done to my coiffure until I actually had to sit with people I knew, and they just kept staring at my head in rapt fascination.

It took months to get that haircut straightened out. The first place that tried was a real Supercuts in Fayetteville, Arkansas. The manager of the store came over and examined my head closely, without touching it. Then she picked up a comb and gently combed a couple of places, watching the hair move through the comb. Finally, she stepped back and looked me in the eye, and said, "You have to tell me the truth. We didn't do that to your head, did we?"

For all the crowding, I do like California. I had two people shake my hand on that day, which is something that rarely happens in my northeastern neck of the woods. One old guy came up when I was getting things together after the haircut. He told me he was an actor and a musician, and played all the small theaters on the west coast. Said he always wanted to get a bike and ride it, but never did. I said you're never too old, but he disagreed. I told him about my trip and he was really impressed, wished me well and shook my hand. What a nice guy.

A little while later I went down to the beach to check my voice mail and call Lucy, and when I was back at the bike a guy and his wife/girlfriend came up, and he started asking questions. He walked around the bike and checked it out thoroughly. When he saw the license plate, he hollered, "Hey honey, this guy rode all the way from New Hampshire!" He said he really admired what I was doing, and wished me a safe journey and a good ride home. And shook my hand.

I rode down Route 1 for quite a while, enjoying the ride, then saw the turnoff for Highway 84 to La Honda, and I had to take it. La Honda was made legendary by Tom Wolfe in The Electric Kool-Aid Acid Test, since it was once the stomping grounds of Ken Kesey. I was hoping a dayglo tree would jump out at me, but no such luck. I did wind up driving past Kesey's old ranch, but I didn't know where to find it. I know now, since I looked it up--it was 7940 La Honda Rd, Rt. 84. I turned off on Old La Honda Road, and put some miles on a skinny, one-lane back road through even more redwoods. I can see why people like it here; and why Kesey liked it.

I always admired his writing. One Flew Over the Cuckoo's Nest and Sometimes a Great Notion were both literature that kept me busy in high school when I was supposed to be reading something else. Then one time, fifteen or twenty years ago, I went to a reading at a local college and actually met the man. I hung back afterwards and chatted with him for a few minutes, something about fighting the good fight, or something, and I got him to sign my old hardcover copy of Sometimes a Great Notion. He wrote in it, "To Paul, Fight Smart! Ken Kesey" with a silver paint marker.

I will always regret that instead of leaving, I should have said, "Hey, what are you doing afterwards? Want to get something to eat?" But I hurried home, and if I hadn't I bet you I could brag now, "Hey, I partied with Ken Kesey one time!"

I can vouch for what many have said, that he did glow with charisma. True, he was not conventionally handsome, but he had an air about him. He was one of the most radiantly charming men I've ever met, the same sort of vibe you'd expect to get from the Dalai Lama. He's gone now, sadly; he just couldn't make that body fly quite as high as his mind.

Time was catching up, and I wanted to spend the night in Steinbeck country, so I headed for the freeway and made a beeline to Salinas. I found the Steinbeck museum first and took the tour. Interesting, but not as satisfying as his writing. I saw Rocinante, his camper from Travels With Charley, and that was neat. Pretty much the first pickup camper ever made.

It was getting on towards 3:00 and still no lunch, so I found my motel and checked in, and had some peanut butter and crackers. I had to try for Big Sur, just to see it, so I fueled up and made a run for it, through Monterey and Carmel traffic on a Friday afternoon. Holy shit. Finally got out of the traffic outside Carmel. The coast typically beautiful, a brilliant blue sea with a rocky shoreline, but there was five times as much traffic as I remembered. Big Sur was disappointingly jammed, not even any place to park. I drove through and back, and then returned to Monterey.

It's too bad. The seascapes on the PCH between Monterey and Big Sur are epic, and Big Sur is the jewel in the crown. Imagine a rocky coast broken up here and there by sand beaches; occasionally you'll see sea lions lounging on the tide line, sea otters floating on their backs in the kelp. Blue-green water with foaming white waves, breaking on beach and rocks, washing over rock ledge that in places juts out into the sea. On these pieces of ledge there are various holes and fissures, and when you walk on them at low tide all these little pools are populated with a vast array of sea life. Anemones, sea urchins, baby octopi, small crabs, seahorses and much more. These tide pools are the places where Ed Ricketts, Steinbeck's "Doc" from Cannery Row, gathered his specimens to sell to other labs, and they're just the same as Doc left them. It's a wondrous place, incredibly scenic from the road, and fascinating up close.

I wanted to stay, and spend more time with the ghosts of Steinbeck's world, but all the dominoes had been laid out in place, and I felt like the first one had already been kicked over. It felt so good to be back here in this beautiful place, but I felt like I had hacked and slashed all my way getting there, like a swordfight in those old pirate movies, and I was just about too worn out to appreciate it. I felt bad, but I'd just have to come back, and bring a little more energy with me next time. That's not such a bad thing.

Once back in Monterey, I found Cannery Row, which is nothing more than a strip-mall souvenir area now, but I was starving and went to El Torito for supper. Back when I lived in California, El Torito was one of my favorite Mexican chain restaurants, so I had to go. But this time, the food was disappointing. The restaurant was right on the water, though, which is where I wanted to be. It was good to see the Pacific one more time. I had made my decision. In the morning I would turn towards the east and start heading home.

John Steinbeck's camper, Rocinante. Salinas, California.

It was hard to be silently philosophical in a noisy restaurant full of tourists in a busy town full of traffic, but I was well aware I was at the crux moment of the trip. This was it. This was the point where instead of "going away" I was going to be "coming back." I was of two minds, as I picked at my enchiladas and tried to resist the tide that was obviously starting to come back in. I had scooted across the country on a wave, it felt like, and I could turn left here in Monterey or keep going straight down to southern California and my old stomping grounds. I wasn't really sure what I should do, and all the noise and confusion around me didn't help.

Truth was, I was exhausted; and even more than fatigued, I was just plain tired of being on the road. I knew if I went south I would have to add at least two weeks to the length of the trip, it would take that or more to make the rounds. There were many people I would want to visit, some I felt I had to visit, and I'm sure some I would visit without knowing I wasn't really welcome. But that's the way it is; and there would also be a lot of locations I would want to at least ride by. Like the citrus groves in Ojai, hoping to smell the orange blossoms again. Like the location of the old Indian Dunes motocross track, a place I spent half my time, it seems, back in the days when I worked for Dirt Bike magazine. Definitely I would want to explore all the piney-wooded back roads between San Luis Obispo and Frazier Park. Maybe my old house, or my old apartment building where I started my "California trip" back in 1976. Once there, I could think of dozens more places I'd want to see, as well as that long list of people.

But there just wasn't time, or maybe money. Or maybe I was lacking patience. I might have been leaving a few things undone, a few places unexplored, but it was time to start thinking about getting off the road. And there was a long ride ahead, between here and there.

8/21/10 Saturday

At 7:00 I was up and out, heading north on 101 looking for breakfast. I felt a certain amount of regret when I turned east off the highway but spiritually I was ready to be headed home. From the early days of living there, I have a lot of memories of California, but none of them include the vast numbers of people I found on this trip—though in the old days I did complain about the crowds. I was ready to go back to my peaceful little house in New Hampshire, knowing that my picture of the world out there is a better and quieter one than really exists.

I had another sad realization, first thing in the morning. As I got on the freeway in Salinas, I passed an In-N-Out Burger just a few blocks away from where I had been staying. Now, in case you don't know, In-N-Out Burger is a California fast-food shrine, home of arguably the finest wax paper-wrapped cheeseburger known to man. The true believers, of which I am one, don't need further convincing, but among other things In-N-Out played a big part in the movie The Big Lebowski. I got hooked on In-N-Out in the '70s when I was living in California, and since there aren't any franchises east of Texas I don't get to see them much. So what this meant was, as I was starving, eating peanut butter the day before, I could have been gorging myself with California's finest. I was miserable until well past noon, thinking about it.

I had been keeping cool since Oregon thanks to the bank of ever-present ocean clouds well known as the "marine layer." The marine layer stayed with me up until Gilroy, the "Garlic Capital of the World," and once over the pass it stayed behind on the hills. Shreds of it blew over--it was trying to follow me, but topography is something you just can't fight. The hills held the clouds back; that's just where they belong, staying back on the Pacific keeping the Bay Area cold and damp. Mark Twain once said that the coldest winter he ever spent was a summer in San Francisco, and if you ever spend some time there, you'll understand what he meant.

The central valley was sunny and a little warmer, but it was still zipped-up sweatshirt weather until I got to the hills on the far side. Then the heat started increasing, and it got much drier. Soon it was well past 90 degrees, and I shed all coastal clothes down to a T-shirt. I followed the Merced River up onto the Yosemite Highway, and all that moving water looked real inviting. By the time I got within sight of the entrance gate to Yosemite I'd made up my mind, and I turned around and found a spot on the river to take a swim.

Air temp must have been near 100 degrees, and I was cooked by the time I stopped. There were a few people there, one fairly entertaining Jerry Garcia replica, but everybody kept to themselves. I'd noticed on my ride up that it seemed that a number of the girls dipping in the river preferred to do it topless, but there were none of that persuasion where I went in. Unfortunately. Nice cool water, just deep enough to get submerged a little, and soak off the heat. After an hour I got back on and headed into the park.

When I lived in California, Yosemite was one place I never visited. I'm a huge Ansel Adams fan, so I had a vision of a Yosemite that was maybe, umm, a little dated. Like maybe from the '40s, when only a few hardy souls would make the trip, and Adams was just a local goofball with a big camera.

Well, there is still a lot of very impressive geography deep down in Yosemite Village, but there are so many people you can't see anything. Thousands and thousands of people, very few of them speak English, most of them appear to be Chinese or Japanese tourists. Everywhere you go, there is a line to stand in. Everything you want to look at, hundreds or thousands of people want to see it too. It was my third huge National Park of the trip, and my third disappointment. If you came to Yosemite in October or November, maybe it would be a nicer place. But in the high season, do yourself a favor and stay home.

Well, I had made arrangements to stay in Yosemite Village, for the sake of convenience. I was going to get there late, and I knew there wasn't much outside of Yosemite for lodging. I had a reservation in a place called the Housekeeping Village, the only thing they had available, and it was highly recommended by the person on the phone. After I arrived I parked and walked through the crowds until I found the place to register in the Village, and finally found my Housekeeping Unit. As far as I could tell it was just a fancy name for a refugee camp. It was very dusty and dirty, and the accommodations consist of a three-sided concrete shelter with a canvas roof and a sort of canvas shower curtain on one end. There were electric lights, but any romance is spoiled by the presence of many, many other people talking and shuffling around, in and out of their cars, and dozens of dirty children running around in the dark kicking up great clouds of dust, and also making considerable noise.

Every "camp" of the hundreds here also had to have its very own campfire, of course, whether anyone was sitting around it or not. I couldn't imagine why they would want to, since even after dark the air temperature was way up in the high 80s. Consequently, there were dozens of unattended firepits with smoldering, smoking green logs in them, and since there was no air moving in the valley, the whole place was slowly filling up with smoke. And dust from the kids running around. Refugee camp. Can you tell I don't like "camping?"

The other odd thing about Yosemite Village is that you can't hardly see any of the things you've seen in the pictures. It's all there, but you're down low in a valley, looking up at it. My feeling is that you could appreciate everything better from a certain amount of height, but in my short visit I hadn't figured out how to get to that position. I had hopes that an early morning start would get me up to where the views might be.

Not to continue with the negativity or anything, but as I sat in the Yosemite Lodge waiting for my $17 cheeseburger, I noticed that the walls of the restaurant were covered with photos of the local nature. Some of them were near-knockoffs of some of the works Ansel Adams created during his lifetime. Right in front of me, on the opposite wall of the restaurant, was another "Oak Tree in Snowstorm" done by another photographer, but there was no card identifying who. It was the same oak tree Adams used, different snowstorm I'm sure, and the composition was slightly different. It was a color photo, as opposed to Adams' original black and white photo, and very pretty. Just about perfect in lighting and composition, etc., very dramatic in the way it used light and color. But it made me wonder what Ansel Adams gets out of it. Most people might say this new photo was much better, but is it true? Is an Adams photo better? Does he just get kudos for being the first? Or is an Adams photo just a dull black and white version of the scene, as aged as the rest of us? Does it really have as much value as people think, or is it just an anachronism; photography from a different time? Does photography last as long as the Old Masters, or does something newer and better eclipse it?

I don't know. It's hard to say with photography. I looked at the Ansel Adams photos for sale in the gallery. Originals, I would assume printed by him, are priced at $9,000 to $12,000 or more. Reproductions, from his original negatives but printed by an assistant of his, can be had for as little as $225. But then, this same assistant has his own original photos there for sale as well, some from almost the same "tripod holes" as Adams, and his photos, technically perfect, are available for about $1000.

Where do you draw the line? Did Adams' photos turn into art when he took the picture, or only when he printed his interpretation of the negative? Is his original photo really worth less because someone else who was taught by him and prints to the same technical standards printed it after the fact? And what about duplications of the same scene, with even greater range and fidelity and more careful composition--are they valuable as well, or just copycat? It's an awful tough call.

And no, I didn't hunt down Ansel Adams' "Oak Tree" to try to duplicate his work with my little Olympus pocket camera. Hell, it wasn't even snowing.

And as I mused about this the kids continued stomping the dust into great clouds, and my tent filled with smoke and dirt. My plan was to leave early in the morning, before they all got up and threw more shit in the firepits. The one thing I know about Ansel Adams' work is that when he took his photos he was gloriously alone, just him and his big sheet-film camera. I think he'd be rolling in his grave if he could visit Yosemite now.

Big rock, Yosemite, California.

In Bodie Ghost Town, California.

8/22/10 Sunday

I escaped from the refugee camp at dawn. I had to find someone from the housekeeping staff and plead with them to take my sheets and blankets, since you have to return them yourself and they don't open at a decent hour. I grabbed a very quick breakfast out of one of the food troughs set aside for the masses, and got on the bike. I did stop on the way out to gaze at the great wall of Half Dome, this time seeing it without having to look over a sea of black hair.

I left the park to the east, on the Tioga Road, and it was still early in the a.m. It was warm already, and my Gore-Tex was sticking to me. I had left without showering because the facilities in the refugee camp were scary. You were issued a ticket that would allow you past the guard into a filthy shower facility, following in the footsteps of hundreds of other unfortunates. Gosh, I hate to sound fussy, but there was nothing picturesque about the place.

The good part about leaving early was getting out before the tourists, so I enjoyed a fine morning's ride in the cooler air, the smell of evergreens and dry pine needles on the breeze. The Tioga Road is a very scenic two-lane highway across the eastern Sierras. In the view of an Easterner, it's amazing how much bare rock there is; and the view is much more satisfying, since you're looking down at it rather than up. Tioga Road is the only way to get to Tuolumne Meadows on wheels, a gorgeous place on the far eastern side of Yosemite Park. All in all, I guess Yosemite is worth a visit, just don't expect too much. Especially don't expect solitude with your scenic grandeur.

The road descended down to Lee Vining and Route 395 in California. It was a great ride, and very impressive through the rocky Tioga Pass. A quick left at the bottom takes you to Mono Lake, so I had to head up there, and signs along the way told about Bodie Ghost Town, which I'd never seen and figured I'd better do it. Bodie is one of those places where the ore ran out after a promising start, and as soon as the word got out just about everybody left. When Bodie was booming the residents spared no expense to build a town that was going to be home for quite a while. When it busted they ran off in search of the next score, and left everything standing just like it was.

It's a mind-boggling place. Many of the buildings have been cleaned up a little and put back in order, but the story was clear—most folks just left everything behind. Some of the stores look like they've been minimally re-stocked since then, but even the run-down places still have furniture and junk inside. Such was the effects of gold fever, I guess. It was easy enough to get anything you wanted when the mines were working, so just drop everything and rush to the next place before everyone else. A most strange little ghost town, but a delightful way to spend a couple hours.

I talked to one of the rangers on duty, and found out that Forest Service employees who work there are housed in some of the old cabins, ones that have been fixed up and presumably have propane or generators for some sort of power and light. There are one or two little "neighborhoods" in Bodie where the workers live, which must help cut down on vandalism. This particular ranger, a young woman, did admit that occasionally they might just do some partying there in Bodie, after all the tourists leave. I can only imagine how much fun it must be to be stumbling around drunk in a ghost town!

Again, I was torn with all sorts of potential destinations that day. It was only a short hop from Bodie to Lake Tahoe, but I had been there fairly recently on a business trip, and didn't really feel the need. I would have liked to wander down Route 395 on the California side, and visit Mammoth Lakes, where I had spent some time skiing way back when. Or roll farther down, to Bishop, and try to catch a glimpse of Mt. Whitney, California's highest peak. Or even continue down 395 and go into the Mojave Desert proper, as far down as Death Valley. Umm...in August?

Ultimately, I turned back and scooted down Route 120, then to Route 6 and into Nevada, to the town of Tonopah as it got hotter and hotter. Maybe the temperature went up to 95 degrees, not too bad for a desert in August, but after a week of cold mist it felt sweltering.

I was heading for the Mizpah Hotel in Tonopah, the first place west of the Mississippi to get an elevator. I've had some good times in the Mizpah, way back in the misty past, and would have loved to get one of their old Victorian rooms, with a view out the front, but alas the Mizpah was closed. Still closed, since it was in the same condition the last time I was in Tonopah. The hotel was built in 1905, annexed onto the Mizpah Saloon, built 1901, which was the first permanent structure in Tonopah. The saloon and hotel took their name from the Mizpah Mine, of course, which provided the finances for the town. The hotel was the social center of Tonopah back in it's heyday, and it is just a gorgeous, funky building. When I was last there, we spent time at the old bar that dominates the entire first floor. From there you could take the elevator—not many more than two people can fit in it—or the winding dark oak stairs to the upper floors. It was, and is, I suppose, all Victorian colors and carpeting, tired beds and worn furniture that I wish could recite the history it has seen. Every year, the rumor goes around that the new owners are planning to re-open the place, and I do hope it happens one of these years.

No Mizpah this trip, but I did stay next door at the Jim Butler Inn and got the best room of the trip. The room was the same shape as any other motel room, but outfitted with a nice couch and easy chair, a fake fireplace and a screen between the "living room" and the bed. All the linens in the room were fine quality and homey, not what you usually see in a typical motel. The folks at the Jim Butler were friendly and very accommodating, and I'll have a hard time choosing the next time I'm there, if the Mizpah does re-open.

(Editor's note: The Mizpah has been renovated and reopened, as of 2013, which was the next time this writer had a chance to visit Tonopah. Still couldn't get a room there, as it was full. Information on this fine old establishment can be found at themizpahhotel.com.)

The Mizpah, and the Jim Butler Inn, Tonopah, Nevada.

Visiting the Little A'le'inn, Rachel, NV.

8/23/10 Monday

I should have stayed an extra day in Tonopah. I should have done a number of things differently, but I had the itch to keep moving south. I had arranged to visit some friends down in southern Arizona, and considering the heat I was going to be facing I figured it's better to get after it, rather than dawdle.

I rolled out of Tonopah early in the morning, before the heat. Got breakfast at the Station Hotel, filled the bike to the top with fuel and hit the road. The temperature was nice and cool. I mused on a great idea--that I should win the lottery for about 180 million and then come back and buy Tonopah. Just buy the whole town. Fix up the Mizpah and the Hotel Belvada across the street. Put in a world class shooting venue, and fix up the bowling alley, make the town a bowling and competitive shooting destination. Golf wouldn't work, it takes too much water. I have such good ideas when I'm riding alone. Too bad I don't have incredibly deep pockets.

Somewhere in the morning the odometer passed 10,000 miles. I calculated the mileage at the gas station in the morning, and the bike was still getting 48 mpg consistently. Good thing, too. From Tonopah, up Route 6, and then off onto 375, the Extraterrestrial Highway to Rachel, there is no gas available. The closest gas is in Caliente, which works out to be just about 200 miles. Almost the limit of the bike. I guess theoretically the bike can go almost 250 miles, but I've never taken it past 230. At that, the gas gage is freaking out.

Cool air prevailed all across Nevada, and the riding was fun and easy. At Warm Springs I turned off onto the famed Extraterrestrial Highway, northeast of the also famous "Area 51" and Groom Lake, and headed for the town of Rachel. Rachel is the home of the Little A'le'in, a little roadside rest with the distinction of being the center of the earth for UFO conspirists everywhere. There's no fuel available at Rachel, but you can get an Alien Burger and fries. And your chances of being abducted are actually fairly low.

I had forgotten how immense Nevada is, how much space the state has. I do like it there, and without a doubt Tonopah is my favorite burg. I'll be torn between living in Washington State and northern Nevada, if I ever relocate to the far side of the country.

At the end of the Extraterrestrial Highway, it's still another 43 miles to Caliente, and by the time I arrived I was looking for the first gas station I saw, happy that the bike didn't start hiccupping at the town line. I bought a bottle of water at the gas station and downed it, then parked at a burger joint and got a little lunch and enjoyed some air conditioning. It was hot out, but not so bad; and I had thoroughly enjoyed the morning's ride.

Caliente was a familiar place, as I'd been there a number of times before. Two or three times during the Nevada Rally series in the mid-'90s, during a couple of dual sport rides at about the same timeframe, and at least once for the Nevada 200 trail ride. In spite of all this familiarity, I just don't feel comfortable there. For no rational reason, I feel like a wanted man in Caliente. It must be some sort of a past life experience. Whatever it is, I got my business done and quickly got out of town.

Coming into Utah the air temperature went up, but it was moderate, being late afternoon. I arrived in Cedar City and wasn't impressed, and decided to keep going another hour to Kanab. That would be one hour less I'd have to ride the next morning, if the weather decided to get real hot. Still worried about the heat, I thought if it did get severely hot, I'd ride in the early morning and then get a room and hide out for the afternoon. It even crossed my mind to see if the smaller hotels will do an afternoon rate, and leave for a few more hours riding maybe at 4:00 or so, especially for the final push to Arkansas.

It might sound foolish to spend so much time worrying about air temperature, but hammering along at 70 mph into a 100 degree wind is like riding straight into a blow drier. I kept the jacket on just to try to maintain a little moisture, and I do believe it helped. I kept thinking about the German girl Jutta Kleinschmidt, who rode one of the Nevada Rally events zipped up tight in a Dainese riding jacket, while all the rest of us were suffering in 100 degree sun. She must have been baking inside of that thing, but we probably weren't much cooler, and she swears it helped her stay hydrated. But jacket on or off, I'm just not partial to the heat. And I don't mind complaining about it, either.

I decided to skip Bryce and Zion National Parks, and the Grand Canyon. Been there before. As fun as this trip has been, I was starting to smell the barn, and was itching to get back to Lucy's house and take a break. Hard as it may be to believe, public restrooms had lost all their charm.

Deciding to skip to Kanab rather than Cedar City turned out to be one of those fortunate events that you can't predict. Wandering down Kanab's main street, I spotted the Parry Lodge motel and decided that was the place to stay. Why? Because it was single-story, painted white, and built in the grand old tradition of southeastern road-motels, with white columns and multi-light windows. It just looked good. Plus, there was plenty of neon in the sign.

Little did I know that I had just wandered into the nerve center of Little Hollywood. I sweet-talked the lady behind the desk into a good rate for a weary traveler, and she did the paperwork and handed me a key. "You're staying in Arlene Dahl's room, honey," she said.

"Who?"

"Arlene Dahl. Haven't you seen the map?" she asked, pushing a room map in front of me. "You're right next to Telly Savalas and Tyrone Power."

I stared at the map, and every room of the hotel was named after a certain movie star from long ago. "Did all these people stay here?"

"Are you kidding, honey? This is Little Hollywood. Everybody stayed here."

I looked down the row of room names. "You me to tell me, I could have stayed in Frank Sinatra's room?"

"Not for what you're paying, sugar."

Frank Sinatra's old room was right down the row. And up at the end, it was Dean Martin and Sammy Davis Jr. And I got Arlene Dahl? Think of the mojo I missed out on!

But it was a great place. Nice little rooms, everything clean, and 8:00 each night they play a free movie for guests in the barn out back. I went in and watched a Western called The Fargo Kid, starring Tim Holt, whoever he was. I'm not even sure the movie was a "talkie," thinking back. Kanab is a cool place, though. The legend is that the guys who originally opened the Parry Lodge did a lot of promotion in Hollywood, where all the Western movies were being made at the time, and convinced many of the studios that they could make more realistic Westerns right out here in Kanab, where all the amenities were available, etc. They came in droves, and Kanab really was Little Hollywood for many years. You still can ride a few miles out of town and see the old movie sets, withering in the sun. And of course the Parry Lodge has everyone's photo up on the wall.

The sun sets on the Parry Lodge in Little Hollywood, Utah.

8/24/10 Tuesday

This day was a fairly uneventful, from Kanab to Prescott, AZ. Pretty much with the sun in my eyes all the way to Arizona, so I didn't see much. I stopped at Johnson Ranch Road outside Kanab to take a photo of one of the movie sets left over from the old days. I have to watch The Outlaw Josie Wales one more time and see if I recognize the landscape.

Stopped for a while at Glen Canyon Dam. Very impressive. Utah is all cliffs and canyons, monstrous, monumental landscapes everywhere you look. I decided I would have gone to the Grand Canyon after all, if I had one more day. But I didn't. Plus, every ten miles south I rode it seemed to get another degree hotter. My imagination? I'm not too sure.

My plan at this point was to head south, down to Maricopa, below Phoenix, to visit my old friend Rick, a.k.a. Super Hunky. The Hunk was expecting me, more or less, but that wasn't really the cause of my haste, at this point. I knew I had at least a two-week break waiting for me in Arkansas, and since I had been on the road every day for the past two weeks, since Washington, that was a powerful incentive. And again, I was seriously concerned about the heat I was running into with this southbound diversion. I had visions of the clear, cool air of the North Dakota prairie running through my head as I headed farther south

Once I hit Arizona, I turned off to Tuba City to buy fuel and get another bottle of cold water. This is all Navajo Indian country, and a painted plywood sign by the side of the road promised dinosaur footprints, so I turned off and stopped. Footprints, bones, skulls, skeletons, petrified eggs and excrement were just laying around on the desert floor. Now I know that the things we used to joke about being dinosaur bones, when we were out riding in the desert, really were. If you know what you're looking for, you can see it pretty easily.

Now this was my idea of a nature area. No stern green-uniformed wool-hatted authority figure standing around telling you what you can't do. No snack bars, souvenir shops or refugee camps full of tourists to deal with. Just dinosaur bones scattered over a few acres of bare desert terrain, and a group of Indian guys and gals to point things out—and sell you jewelry. It's all on Indian land, so the National Park Service can't throw a fence around it and charge you admission—or for that matter, keep you out altogether. A laconic Navajo guy showed me around, and then waited for a tip. I gave him $10 and bought a couple polished stone bracelets.

From there the road was dead south, and with every ten miles it got hotter and hotter. I tried to call Rick early in the afternoon, from outside of Flagstaff, to see if I could show up later that day, but with no luck. I kept going, rather than stopping in Flagstaff. The road ran straight south and downhill, and as I descended it became alarmingly hotter. I finally stopped south of Prescott in 100 degree heat. This time I got hold of Rick. He was headed to a poker tournament, and strongly suggested that I stay right where I was and make a run for Maricopa in the early morning. He said it was 107 in Maricopa, and 109 in Phoenix. Rick had a good idea.

So I headed back into Prescott and found suitable lodging, and another Mexican restaurant for supper. Again I suffered time-confusion until I found out that Arizona doesn't recognize Daylight Savings Time. I thought I had slipped back into Pacific time for a short while there.

Dinosaur bones near Tuba City, AZ.

8/25/10 Wednesday

I got up early and rode down to Maricopa, and surprised Rick by riding right to his house. Hey, I know how to navigate! Rick and I used to work together back in the early '80s, both on the staff of Dirt Bike magazine. He is still largely the same as he was back in his prime—a fleshy face with handlebar moustache, dark-rimmed glasses, muscular build, and a surprising lack of grey hair. Rick is an amazing guy, who can be extremely well-informed in every facet of some things, and totally clueless in others. Case in point was our first conversation as soon as I arrived. He knew I was headed there on a motorcycle, and when I pulled into his garage and stopped he took one look at the Suzuki and said, "Clip—this is a street bike!"

"Well, Rick," I said, "it would be damn awful hard to do it on a dirt bike. What did you think I was riding, a Hodaka?"

"Well, I didn't know...I didn't think about it. A street bike!"

I spent the rest of the day hiding out in the air conditioning, and not riding the bike. The street bike! Only Rick could assume, somewhere in his head, that I was naturally riding a dirt bike around the United States. We met Rick's wife Tina after work, at a Chinese buffet that was the best I've ever been to. They had frog legs!

8/26/10 Thursday

Another merciful day of no riding. Hot again, into the hundreds, although thunderstorms wandered through the valley. Following up on a previous invitation, Rick and I drove down to Ed Hertfelder's house in Tucson, almost a two-hour drive. I had been invited to stay with Hertfelder for as long as I liked, rooming in his daughter's house, but since leaving California I had tipped over to the other side, and now I was anxious to get back east. It's hard to put a label on exactly what it is that sends us back the way we came, maybe a form of homesickness. But more realistically, I was dog-tired and my enthusiasm for being on the road was draining away like coolant from a holed radiator. I knew that Ed was disappointed I wasn't going to stay, but home, or at least familiar terrain, was calling me.

In truth, it was a situation that was already affecting the trip. I had wanted to spend more time in Nevada. I wanted to do a loop; head from Tonopah up to Austin, then to Elko and come back down through the Ruby Mountains to Ely, then Panaca, and then take 319/56 down into Arizona. This Nevada loop was planned even before the trip started; I could even make an argument that it was one of the basic reasons for the whole trip. I've been around Nevada before; three times with the Nevada Rally back in the early '90s, and on a couple of dual sport trips. I'm familiar with all these towns in Nevada, absolutely love the place, and just wanted to go back this time for a lingering visit. Instead, I'd already zipped through the state in just half a day, because I was running out of patience. That's what happens when you're road weary, and it was destined to bother me for some time—obviously until the time came when I could ride back there.

(Editor's note: I did go back and do that long, lazy loop in Nevada, three years later on a BMW GS1150, in the fall of 2013. I bought the bike from a friend of a Dorian's in Washington, and rode it down through the Sierras and had a fine old time. That was the next big ride, and it ended in Denver, where I put the bike into storage for the winter. Considering it was only a ten day trip or so, I doubt I'll ever write about it. But it was fun!)

But now we were in Arizona, in Tucson, Hertfelder's stomping grounds. Ed looks the same, with his bald head, thick glasses and goatee; and he's looking lean and fit for his 80 years. It was a summit of sorts, me and Ed and Rick; you could almost call it three generations of moto-journalists. How about three half-generations?

Ed's girlfriend Beverly joined us for lunch, and we had a good afternoon of chatting and eating, telling stories. Fun stuff. I don't even remember any of the stories we told, seriously. I think we just skimmed the surface. For all our occupational similarities, you couldn't really pick three more different people. Three writers of completely different mindsets. Hertfelder, the old guard, still remembers when riding enduros on a Harley was the only way to be competitive. Rick, the Youngstown, Ohio-to-California transplant who is still very much a motocross and desert racer. And then there's me—and I have no idea how to categorize myself. Modern post-vintage retired enduro rider? We told our tales, though, as best we could; and had a good time, however brief.

Rick and I drove back to Maricopa afterwards, fighting our way through thunderstorms in his ratty old pickup truck with non-working windshield wipers. Why fix the wipers when it never rains in Arizona? Some things never change.

We picked up some oil for the V-Strom at a bike shop on the way, and walked in side by side. I'm sure we both would have been pleased if the guy in the shop had said, "Hey, aren't you two...?" But it didn't happen. They didn't know us from any other old bums on the street. I changed the oil in the bike when we got back to Rick's, and made preparations to make a run for it in the cool of the morning.

Ed Hertfelder and Rick Sieman, Tucson, Arizona, August 26, 2010.

8/27/10 Friday

There were thunderstorms to the west as I left Maricopa at 7:00, but it was still trying to be hot wherever the sun came out. The fact that I had seen no other motorcycles on the road in Arizona was not lost on me. Being on that bike, in Arizona in August, was like being the ant under the magnifying glass.

I followed the map to Chandler and up to Superior, AZ, where I had breakfast at the Los Hermanos restaurant. Superior looked interesting, another dried up western town with a lot of closed-up shops. Downtown looked like a ghost town.

Heading east from there the temperature changed with the altitude, and within 20 miles I was zipped up tight in my jacket, and stayed that way almost the whole day. Merciful heavens. It was cloudy, cool, and even rainy at times, as I skirted by a few small thundershowers. I rode route 60 through eastern Arizona and past the New Mexico border, and the countryside was beautiful. Canyons and mesas gave way to rolling green grasslands. The road is mostly straight, not very interesting, and I kept the speed up because I wanted to burn away the miles between there and Arkansas.

A little before lunchtime, Route 60 took me up into Pie Town, New Mexico, and you know that if there's pie, that'll make it my second-favorite small town in America. Nothing sounded better at that point than a cup of coffee and a slice of pie.

You see, I come from a long line of pie makers. My mother had a penchant for baking pies, and from watching her at an early age I tended to develop the skill as well. My sister is a pie baker, and so is Lucy. To me, the best thing you can do with any kind of fruit is make a pie out of it—blueberry pie, apple pie, banana cream pie, strangleberry pie, whatever it is, it doesn't make life worth living until it has a crust around it. So when I saw "Pie Town" on the map, I made it a point to roll that direction.

I stopped at the Pie-O-Neer Café, where a guy unfurling the "OPEN" flag and sprucing up the entryway greeted me and invited me in. The Pie-O-Neer was a wood-sided building, vertical log planks, with a deep porch and a false front on the roof, just as you'd expect in a cowboy town. The siding was all dark brown and weathered, but the door frame and trim was painted a bright turquoise blue. As far as a town goes, Pie Town didn't look like much outside of the Pie-O-Neer. There were maybe four other buildings on Highway 60, the rest of the town must have been tucked away on a side street. I slowly got off the bike and took my gear off, helmet on the seat and jacket draped over that. It was bright and sunny, not terribly hot yet, but the shade on the porch looked inviting.

I went inside at sat at the counter, next to the man who greeted me outside. His name was Stan, and he worked on finishing a great looking bowl of soup as I ordered peach pie and coffee. Stan was somewhere around my age, tall and thin and ponytailed; a comfortable looking guy who was a friendly, easy talker. I assumed pretty quickly that he was the husband or partner of Kathy, who was the pie lady.

Kathy busied herself with getting the pies out and the counter tidied, since they had just opened as I pulled up out front. Dressed in loose jeans and a long sleeve T-shirt and covered with a full kitchen apron, Kathy was setting a busy but unhurried pace between the kitchen and the dining room. She covered up a tangle of dirty blond curls with a white baker's toque, and beamed out a hundred watt smile that could melt the heart of a ceramic lawn jockey. She was pretty, outgoing, and possessed that rare kind of charm that surrounds you like a warm burst of humid air on a cold winter day, when you open the door on that oven full of pies. I'm sure they think it's all about the pie, but I'll bet a lot of the guys come into the Pie-O-Neer just to be near Kathy.

I lingered at the counter for a bit, then went outside to call Lucy. No answer on the first try, typical. She was probably out doing something else and left the phone where she couldn't hear it. I wondered why I even wanted to call. Contact with the outside world, the non-riding world, I guess. I had many miles left in front of me, but no desire to get back on the bike.

I sat on a wicker chair on the front porch of the Pie-O-Neer, and reflected on what I was doing. A small cat, black and white and wide-eyed, appeared at my feet as if on cue. It rubbed its side against my leg and the lower rails of the chair, then jumped into my lap. I scratched its head and thought about what to do next. I was bone-tired; really exhausted, even though I'd spent a couple days doing nothing at Rick's house. I had ridden 300 miles so far that morning alone. Why couldn't I just stay here in Pie Town? I could be happy with a life based on pie.

I thought about heading farther south, down to Roswell and see what the UFO freaks were up to. Or I could explore deep into Texas. The phone rang and I talked to Lucy for a bit. The truth was, the next rest stop was in Arkansas, at her house whenever I got there, and I didn't have to think about it much longer than that.

But fresh in memory was the soup that Stan had been eating. The road fatigue had eased enough that I had finally figured out I was hungry, and just wasn't ready to get back on the bike, so I went back inside and got myself a bowl. I talked to Kathy this time, who was now working on some papers at the lunch counter. She asked where I had come from, where I was headed. I gave her the short version of the story. She took it all in and thought about it for a half a minute, and asked, "Well, now that you're out of the magazine business, what do you want to do next?"

I looked around the room. "You know, I've been thinking about that, and I think I'd like to be a breakfast cook," I told her. "I was in the restaurant business when I was a kid, and I actually liked it a lot."

She nodded thoughtfully at my answer, and her look seemed to go right into my soul.

"Too bad I'm not open for breakfast," she said.

Goll-lee, I love that shit. I had unwittingly handed her a perfect opportunity, and she came back at me with the perfect flirt. We live in a nation of soreheads these days. Everybody is scared to death of everybody else; the hate is so thick in this country you couldn't wash it out of the gutters with a fire hose. And then I get one off-hand flirty line from a lovely woman behind a lunch counter and it was like being hit in the face with a two by four. In this ten-second exchange I might have found what I was hunting for in this whole trip: a simple acknowledgement from a stranger that we were all equals in this disaster called American life.

Plus, it might have been the easiest job interview I've ever had. Even though there was no job.

As I left Pie Town, I promised myself I'd be back some day. Man does not live on peach pie alone. There are many more flavors.

I rode through more gorgeous scenery to Socorro, gave it a pass and drove another 60 miles to Mountainair, NM, because the name sounded refreshing. A billboard somewhere along the road bragged of all the choice motels and restaurants in Mountainaire, so I looked forward to my arrival.

I had started this trip expecting everything from Tonopah to Oklahoma to be a desert, but I couldn't have been more wrong. Of course, southern Nevada was barren, but ever since I had left Arizona I had been following Route 60, and the scenery was mostly as green as could be. It wasn't a wet country, by any stretch of the imagination, but tall trees in dry forests grew in huge patches, interspersed with open prairie land. Occasionally there would be a rocky cliff, or a peak in view, and in Utah I had passed through birch or aspen forests alongside barren lava fields. It wasn't at all what I expected. I was ready for days full of sagebrush and scraggly weeds, and what I found instead was relatively lush.

So far, this was the longest day of the trip, something like 518 miles in the saddle. It introduced me to a new level of fatigue. I did a couple passes through Mountainaire, wondering if the one flea bag motel I saw was the only place to stay, then stumbled onto the historic Shaffer Hotel. They had rooms available and a dining room. Who could ask for more?

The hotel was in a restored Pueblo Deco-style building. Very cool looking place, although somewhat alarming that the exterior was decorated with swastikas. I remembered in my studies somewhere that the swastika is an old symbol, present in Buddhist and Hindu religions, and is actually one of the sacred symbols of Vishnu and represents the rays of the sun. I wondered if it was an accident that the swastika was also a common symbol in Navajo Indian culture, which is obviously where the Shaffer Hotel came across it. Whatever the origin, I was glad to be staying in such a neat place. Well, except for the woman loudly singing out of key karaoke downstairs in the dining room late at night.

I talked to Rick on the phone that evening, and he told me I was lucky to get out when I did. He said 45 minutes after I left, a severe thunderstorm tore through town and uprooted two trees in his neighbor's backyard, before dumping down buckets of rain for half an hour. I told him I had been watching those storms in my rear view mirror as I raced away from Phoenix. Once up on the hills east of the city I could see what was happening behind me, and I stayed on the gas until breakfast that morning, and spent as little time there as I could, just in case. I was learning to not mess with thunderstorms, when I could help it.

At the Pie-O-Neer Cafe, Pie Town, NM.

8/28/10 Saturday

No breakfast, no coffee in the hotel, so I packed up early and went to the restaurant in town. The local guys there for breakfast seemed friendly, but they all talked among themselves. Mostly hysteria about Muslims building mosques, and nudists gathering in town for the weekend. Oh my. No sense hanging around, no joy in seeing nude people unless you can pick which ones.

I was still in the mind of getting away early to beat the heat, and it was becoming imperative to get to Fayetteville and go into rest mode, so I saw no more efficient option than to get on Interstate 40 and tough it out. I hate the slab. It's all trucks and bad drivers, but at least this was a weekend and there were not that many trucks, nor were there daily commuters risking their lives to get to work. It was not a bad drive, out of New Mexico and into Texas, and I was soon in El Reno, Oklahoma, running out of energy and daylight, so that's where I quit.

The next day would be a cruise--only 230 miles to Fayetteville, not much more than three hours of straight-line riding. I had figured the spacing of the days wrong, and finally realized how far I'd gone the day I left Phoenix--518 miles--and then how far yesterday was, about 450 miles. No wonder I felt a mite tired. That's all right, I figured, it would get me to Lucy's place quicker, and then I could take a break.

The only interesting thing about racing across the country on an Interstate is how fast you see the climate change. I started out in low desert, quickly climbed up into high desert and high-altitude arid mountains. Then into prairie, changing quickly into thicker grasslands, then into farming country; and finally, most of the way through Oklahoma, I noticed for the first time lush grasses and weeds, and bushes other than sage and tumbleweed growing alongside the road. This part of the country was suffering a little bit of a drought this particular year, but there was still a huge difference between Oklahoma and Arizona.

Old service station, Mountainaire, New Mexico.

8/29/10 Sunday

I got up early, got breakfast and headed out, anxious to get to Fayetteville, and also anxious to get it done before the heat really started to rise. With the end in sight, the miles went by so slowly. It seemed like I rode ten miles, only to look down and find I'd only gone one. Then I'd wait for another 20 miles and look down to see that I'd moved forward only 1.2 miles more. I am not usually prone to anxious anticipation, but here I was suffering bad.

I was also worrying about the chain, since I could hear the master link starting its ticking noise again. It sounded like a light clunk every second, in top gear at a moderate speed. I went back and forth, thinking I'd leave it alone until I got to my destination and could do it properly, or just put in a new master link on the side of the road. The noise ate its way up to front and center in my brain, and I finally couldn't hear anything else. The roadside won out. I stopped and replaced the link in a few minutes, lubing the new one with chain lube. The old link was definitely dry and worn badly. The clunk disappeared and the bike rolled smoother, and I was able to continue with one less worry.

At ten o'clock in the morning it was already mind-numbingly hot. It didn't help that Route 40 was as boring as blue mud and had more trucks on it than I would have expected on a Sunday. I decided to stay on 40 then take 540 north, just to keep the speed up and avoid having to stop for traffic lights and Sunday local traffic.

I made a tactical error that almost made me run out of fuel on the very last few miles of the day. Gas consumption had gone way up along with the average speed (75-plus), and where I could get 230 out of a tank before, now the warning was coming on at 165 or so. I ignored it on Route 540, thinking I could make it to the house. Only a few miles up 540, the gas gage said "Uh uh" and started flashing at me. Of course, there were no exits or gas station signs for what seemed like a huge number of miles. It started looking serious, so I jumped off the highway at the closest opportunity and followed the GPS to a local gas station. It took 5.1 gallons of gas to fill it, and the V-Strom is said to have a five-gallon tank. I'd say that was cutting it close.

It was just about 11:00 and already over 90 degrees at the gas station. I checked the GPS and it said I had 20 minutes to go, so I called Lucy and told her to open the garage door in ten minutes. I arrived right before noon to a fine reception, and thoroughly glad to be there. For once, I noted down the mileage—12,124 miles total for the trip so far.

Beale Street, Memphis, TN.

9/10/10 Friday

After almost two weeks of resting and eating, plus doing chores around the house, I was finally on the road again. The bike was ready with two new tires. I bought a Bridgestone Trail Wing for the rear and had it mailed in, and I put the front Dunlop 907 back on that I had removed in Washington and then shipped down to Fayetteville. I bought a tube of Never Seize and put the new master link back on, lubed properly, but didn't replace the chain; I figured it was the second chain of the trip, c'mon. It had to go the distance from here.

I also did the usual crazed-manic late-in-the-trip thing of buying a new Sargent seat for the V-Strom, mounted it on the bike and shipped the Suzuki gel seat back home. From my stop in Washington until I arrived in Arkansas, the Suzuki seat had gotten to feel more and more horrible. By the time I stopped for two weeks of rest, I may just as well have been sitting on a cinderblock. I was hoping the Sargent seat would be better (If you'll allow me to jump forward in time, it wasn't that great. I kept it clean and Ebayed it right away when I got home, and went back to the gel seat.)

I was surprised at how exhausted I was when I arrived. For the first week, while Lucy was at work, I usually slept for at least a couple hours every day, aside from sleeping all night. The first day, Monday, I went back to bed after she left for work at ten of seven, and slept 'til noon. That's after a couple of cups of strong coffee! I did the same thing the next day. By the end of the first week I was starting to feel normal again.

Lucy took good care of me. She is a fine cook, and an excellent baker. She kept a steady stream of cakes, cookies, and of course, pies, coming out of the kitchen, and had me fattened back up well past fighting weight by the time I was ready to leave.

Before we left, I wrestled with exactly what I wanted to do. Hard to believe, but a part of me was still nagging at me bad about that loop of Nevada I'd missed. I could skip it, go back some other time. But when was that going to happen? And would it ever happen again? It would only be two days back to Vegas, if I pushed it. Then I could do a loop of Nevada and head back home through Utah and Colorado, Kansas and Missouri. It was a real possibility.

In the end, I decided the trip was getting too long as it was, and I was fairly sure I didn't want to add another week to the journey. Although it would be good...I shelved the idea and decided to continue going east. Another time.

So, we were finally back on the road and heading for Memphis--me, on the bike, and Lucy in her car. It would be a short re-start for the trip, since our plan was to hole up in Memphis Friday and Saturday night and do the tourist thing. We visited Beale Street each night, heard some good music in the BB King Blues Club and had some so-so food, there and in Pig on Beale. We also took the Gibson guitar factory tour, took a tour of Sun Studios, saw the ducks come down at the Peabody Hotel, and of course went to Graceland. Great visit; Memphis is a fun town with lots to do, and friendly residents.

I rode to Memphis by taking Route 16 east through Brashears, then the Pig Trail down to Route 64. Then across 64 all the way to Memphis, which at times was a pain, especially near Little Rock--lots of traffic, lots of people driving too slow. In spite of the traffic, I beat Lucy to Memphis, even though she floored it down the Inter-state.

9/12/10 Sunday

Sunday rolled around and Lucy had to be back at work on Monday morning, so I dragged myself away from both her and Memphis, and set out in an easterly direction. Just to pick up a couple more states on my list, I took Elvis Presley Blvd. south into Mississippi, and then headed east on Route 72. Lots of lights and traffic first, but then it opened up and turned into a good four-lane road, almost absent of cars. I turned north onto the Nachez Trace Parkway instead of going through Muscle Shoals, mostly to save time. The weather was cool and nice for a change, and it was a good ride. Natchez Trace is very scenic, two lanes, no shoulder, with woods or fields on either side of the road. It's like riding through someone's private estate, but slow--the speed limit is 50 mph.

When I got farther north, I swapped the Nachez Trace for Route 64 again, which also turned into a really good road, mostly four lanes and pretty much empty. I decided to ride as much as possible to take advantage of the good weather, so I stayed on the road until 6:30 or so, stopping in Ocoee, TN, just a stone's throw from North Carolina. I passed through Mississippi, Alabama, Tennessee, and just the tip of Georgia on this day. Got a room at the Ocoee Lake Inn for $35, with a family restaurant still open on site. They told me there would be no breakfast in the morning, though. I would have to look down the road.

9/13/10 Monday

With a fairly early start, I stayed on Route 64/74 towards North Carolina, and decided to head for Route 129, the infamous Tail of the Dragon, getting there some time before noon. The Tail of the Dragon is a short section of North Carolina road that is notoriously twisty, something that appeals to motorcyclists because they can try to go faster than they're capable. Risking one's life in this way jolts up the adrenaline like a roller coaster ride. Smart riders—and admittedly more well-heeled riders—buy racing bikes and get their jollies on "track days" at race tracks. Less fortunate riders, and some who can actually afford both, head for places like The Tail and try to treat it like a race track.

This is a bad idea for two reasons. One, there are cars and other bikes coming the other way, sometimes just as recklessly as you are; and two, the speed limit is 30 mph and the police are really interested in making money on the road.

I wish I had read an honest report on The Tail. If I had I wouldn't have wasted my time. The entire road is 29 miles long, but the majority is just typical country road. Then, in the middle, there's what seems like maybe seven miles of twisty stuff, not even all that great. And, as I said earlier, it's posted at 30 mph and crawling with cops with radar.

Oddly, there were three photography businesses set up along the road, taking photos that you could claim on a web site--"Slaying the Dragon." There were quite a number of pseudo-racers on the road, who made it a point to wind first and second gear out to 13,000 rpm when they rode off. There were also plenty of girls in leathers with sport bikes. It's a good road for girls. I got into the twisty stuff, started having a good time, and suddenly the twisty stuff was over, ending in a radar trap and a cop writing speeding tickets.

There are thousands of miles of better riding roads in this country, and most of them are a lot more lightly patrolled. "The Tail of the Dragon" is a great example of the strength of good marketing hype. People come from all over to ride this road; they stay in the local motels and bring their track bikes, working on them like it's a race course. And, some of them actually go away raving about it. What these folks need is a track day to keep them busy. Or, to go up and ride the first 26 miles of the Pacific Coast Highway in California. Now there's a fun road.

I rode through Pigeon Forge and Gatlinburg, just because I'd been there with my kids nearly 20 years ago. Pigeon Forge has eclipsed Gatlinburg in the past 20 years. The place is insane, just a wonderland of out of control commercialism. Amusement parks, mini golf, water slides, museums, arcades—it's like Las Vegas for the post-diaper set. Poor Gatlinburg, in comparison, is a victim of its own original design, and its geography. Gatlinburg was built deep in a ravine, where the climbing hills on either side gave a folksy "down in the holler" look. Well, it looks the same today, because those same hills prevented any expansion for the town. Pigeon Forge had the room, so it spread out. Way out.

My next stop was going to be in Weaverville, NC, home of my friend Len's company, Cyclepedia. Len had been wanting me to visit for years, and now was finally the time. I plotted a route out the back of Gatlinburg and over the hills, and hoped the traffic would thin out. As it turned out, from Gatlinburg to Weaverville was a super-annoying funeral procession all the way. Drivers doing 27 mph in a 55, single lane and oncoming traffic. What a mess. And of course, they all sped up to 70 in the passing zones, only to slow back down to 27 when the road got the least bit curvy. I was ready to pull my hair out when I finally arrived.

9/14/10 *Tuesday*

Tuesday I took another rest day, with a free company tour. Cyclepedia makes their living creating and selling subscriptions to online service manuals for motorcycles. They are unique because they have progressed past the limits of a paper workshop manual. As in, the more photos you print in a paper manual, the more paper you use and the more the final product costs. Cyclepedia has no paper cost to consider, so they can be super-descriptive with their photography. Where a convention manual might only have a few photos of a clutch replacement procedure, for example, a Cyclepedia manual has dozens of photos. And, in this digital age you can look at said manuals wherever you are, with any available comput-

The V-Strom's final service. Cyclepedia Press, Weaverville, NC.

er or with a smart phone or tablet. Very cool stuff.

Greg, the shop mechanic, looked my bike over and told me the chain was shot. I couldn't believe it. He showed me the adjusters—maxed out to the rear, no more adjustment available. Not more than 7000 miles on the second chain of the trip, set up straight and true and adjusted properly. I was now convinced that an o-ring chain was the wrong thing to have on a street bike.

But try to buy one. Greg made some calls and couldn't find a non o-ring chain anywhere. It was going to be another o-ring, and I hated to do it this close to home. We debated the merits of taking a link out and putting it back together with a new master link, but my main fear was that the chain would break on the Chesapeake Bay Bridge-Tunnel. That would not be good.

So we went to the only shop that had a 525 chain in stock—an o-ring chain--and I put on the third chain of the trip. In the end, I had to admit the bike rode smooth again, and was incredibly quiet with the new chain. I just better not plan on putting any more than 7000 miles on it.

9/15/10 Wednesday

This day would begin the final leg of the journey. I was offered an escort for the morning, so we left Weaverville as a group of three. Len was on a Motard KTM 640, Will, one of the writers in the company, was riding a KTM 690SMC. We worked our way out of town and got on the Blue Ridge Parkway, heading north. There was much construction and many small delays on the bottom part of the ride, but the road is far more beautiful than I imagined, having only seen sections of the northernmost half of the Blue Ridge before. This southern part was all new to me, and every turn revealed a new view of craggy canyons and rock-studded cliffs covered with green. More than anything, the bottom of the Blue Ridge reminded me of riding in Europe, through the foothills of the Alps. Really nice. Oddly too, the area is thick with population, but we were nearly alone on the road. The guys explained that by pointing out that the Blue Ridge really doesn't "go anywhere," it's not a through road to get from one populous point to another.

I had been used to grinding out long miles on a trouble-free bike, and I was a little shocked when we had to stop and wait for Will, who had rattled the rear fender off his bike. Len and I were both generous with our abuse, until Len started running out of gas in a particularly remote part of the road. "Well, I thought it was full...." he said, holding his gas cap and peering down into his tank. I just stood and shook my head. They worked on finding the nearest gas station on the GPS, and I abandoned them both to buddy-system their way home.

The Parkway is great. It has a posted speed limit of 45 mph, but for a small local road that's not bad. And it's pretty enough that you don't mind cruising at 50 and playing swivel-head with the scenery. Also on the plus side, there are no stop signs, no traffic lights, no shopping centers, and not really a whole lot of traffic, so it's possible to cover ground pretty quickly. It's also twisty enough that you don't have to ride very fast to have fun. What traffic there is, are people who simply can't drive--Prius owners who slow down to 25 mph anytime there's a curve in the road; then, of course, they speed up to 55-plus in the passing zones. This was becoming a recurrent theme of the trip. Why do they speed up? Why not stay slow and stupid and let people pass them?

I took the Parkway all the way up into Virginia, and then got on Route 58 across southern VA. Route 58 goes right through Axton, VA, home of Gary Bailey. I wish I had noticed that my path was going to lead through Axton, I might have looked him up. Gary is the premier motocross riding teacher in the USA, and a good friend from the old days. I had been to his schools a number of times, even to his track right here in Axton. I thought about beating the bushes and trying to find his house, but I could practically smell the ocean and had to keep going.

Route 58 is a good road, a four-lane rural highway. There is very little traffic and few trucks, but the maximum speed is 60 mph. I just laid back and ground out the miles, doing something more than 400 miles that day, trying to get closer to Cambridge, MD and an easy ride to my mom and dad's place on Thursday. As if the Gods of the Road were watching out for me, I found a Days Inn outside Emporia, Virginia, that had, of course, a Mexican restaurant attached to it. I was in spitting distance of the Chesapeake Bay Bridge-Tunnel, and that would be the main treat on the morrow, as they say. I had a celebratory margarita and some enchiladas, knowing that this was the last motel I'd be pay for on this trip. In three days I'd be sleeping in my own bed again.

9/16/10 Thursday

A discrete puddle of chain lube was the only evidence that I had checked and lubed the chain on the bike the night before, and in the morning I looked everything else over before breakfast. I'd be facing the Bay Bridge-Tunnel in a little less than 70 miles, and though I knew deep inside that it would be a breeze, I figured it would be a good practice to go over the bike just a little to make sure. The last place you'd want to break down on a bike is in a long tunnel. Or on a bridge.

At this point I was still amazed that the V-Strom was as bullet-proof as it had been. Over 13,000 miles on the clock, and no grief to speak of. One broken master link, and one badly connected spark plug lead was all the trouble I'd had. The mysterious "FI" alert and red light on the instrument panel that popped up in Michigan—and recurred occasionally between there and Washington—was a dim memory now. Nothing ever came of it, and nothing else ever went wrong. The bike wore out chains and tires, and otherwise ran like a Swiss watch. Yes, my little 650 hasn't got the horsepower of the 1000cc V-Strom, but I never needed all that displacement, and never missed it.

The ride from Emporia to Virginia Beach was another long stretch, that seemed to take a lot longer than I wanted it to—just like the last leg into Arkansas. I knew the reason all too well—when I arrived at the other side of the Bridge-Tunnel I'd be on familiar roads again. This trip was ending rapidly, and I have to admit I was just about ready for it to be over.

Getting on the bridge was no problem at all. One of the things I did before I left was install an EZ-Pass toll-paying box under the lid of the fiberglass topbox on the bike. I did this, of course, because it's a pain in the ass to stop for tolls, especially on a bike when you're wrapped in Gore-Tex. It worked like a charm, everywhere in the east. I think the only other places I paid a toll were the Mackinac Bridge and the Golden Gate. On both bridges, I just stashed a five-dollar bill in an open jacket pocket and wobbled up to the window. There are so many toll roads and bridges in the east, though, that you don't want to be doing that.

I stopped at the rest area on the Bridge-Tunnel to take some photos, and realized why all the good pictures of it are taken from the air. Trying to capture the essence of that bridge-tunnel from ground level is like trying to get a shot of a submarine from the surface of the water. I gave up after a while and ducked down into the hole and came up the other side on the Delmarva Peninsula. "Delmarva" is a combined name of the states Delaware, Maryland, and Virginia. The fancy name for such a device is a portmanteau; as in, "Delmarva is a portmanteau of three state names." See, now you learned something from this tome.

The 75 miles of Route 13 is the only way to conquer the long strip of Virginia on the other side of the Bridge-Tunnel, and on this trip it didn't seem as bad as it has in the past. You see, 13 has a crossroads about every three to five miles its entire length, and the last time I was there, a number of years back, it seemed like I had to stop at every traffic light, which happened to be at every crossroads. This sort of thing can get annoying. I hit on a lucky timing interval this time, plus there was very little traffic, so I rolled through just about every light. It still seemed to take a long time to get to Maryland, though.

But soon Pocomoke City rolled into view, and then Salisbury, then Cambridge. A short trip through farm fields out to the waterfront, and I was pulling up at my parents' house.

My folks, Harry and Marleen, retired here 30 years ago or so, and spend their time fishing and crabbing, and doing jigsaw puzzles. They live an idyllic life that is only hampered by the usual complaint of octogenarians—not being young any more. They were pleased to see me back, safe and sound, plus my sister Robbie was there, and my cousin Marlene. I wasn't quite home yet, but I was sleeping in familiar surroundings.

9/17/10 Friday

In the morning, we did something predictably loopy. My sister and I hatched a plan the night before that we would cross the state of Delaware and catch one more ferry before it was all over. We'd take the Cape May-Lewes ferry from Lewes, Delaware, over to the tip of the state of New Jersey and have lunch at our favorite place on the Wildwood Boardwalk (Olympic Flame!) and then maybe even take a swim in the ocean. One more boat!

So we raced across the state, me leaving with an only partially full tank of gas, and then the trouble started. Of course, we were trying to catch the same ferry, and knew the time we had to be at the ferry terminal for the 11:00 departure. No problem, I have a bike, I can beat her easily, once I fill it with fuel....

But the first gas station I went to, in Cambridge, the pumps didn't work. Okay, I'll hit the next one. I stopped at the next station I saw, and the card reader didn't work. There was a long line of people at the register, and I didn't want to wait, so I took off and knew I'd stop at the very next station. Trouble is, the area is fairly rural, and the next station was about 20 miles away, and the gas tank kept getting lighter.

No problem, I rolled into the next place, and they were out of gas. How can this be happening? I jumped back on and scooted to the other side of that town, all the while following the GPS on a route I've driven before. I get to the next station, and there's a power failure, and the pumps don't work. So that's four stations I've stopped at so far, and at each one I flop the tank bag back in a well-practiced ritual, and unlock the gas cap. So every time I stop I have to close the cap and flop the tank back and secure it.

Finally, I rolled into the next town with the gas gage blinking like mad, just like it was doing in Arkansas, and the pumps work. But the card reader doesn't work. So I quick throw a ten dollar bill at the register attendant and run over to put ten bucks in. Everything goes without a hitch and I'm out of there, but at this point I've stopped at five gas stations, and it's getting late. I only broke a

One last ferry. Lewes, Delaware, September 17, 2010.

few little traffic laws the last 20 miles to the ferry, but nobody saw me do it, so that's all right.

I got there just as they were loading the last long row of cars onto the ferry. "Can I get on this boat?" I yelled to the cashier.

"Yeah," she said, "if we hurry!"

I bought the ticket in record time and pulled up to the front of the absolute last line. The traffic handler at the end held up his hands to stop me from doing something dumb. He came over and said, "You made it. No trouble now. Are you the guy who's meeting his sister on the boat?"

"Yeah. How do you know about that?"

"Oh everybody knows about it," he replied. "You'll find her, she's already on."

I like it when my imminent arrival is expected. I was the last vehicle there, and true to the traffic guy's word, Rob was at the upper deck rail and I waved to her as I rolled on the boat. Time to get a coffee and watch the Atlantic Ocean roll by the hull.

The Cape May-Lewes Ferry is a fun trip. They're huge ferry boats, carrying up to 100 vehicles at a time. They have comfortable places to hang out inside, and at the height of the summer season they'll have a nice cocktail lounge open on each boat. Or you can sit outside in the breeze, or stand at the rail and watch the dolphins race the wake of the boat. Every summer I try to spend time at the Jersey Shore, so the ferry is an easy way to take a quick visit to see the folks.

The main reason we're down there is body surfing—surfing the waves without the use of a board. It seems like every summer my sister and I are either body surfing or wishing we were. And the older we get, the more intense it seems to get. No, you don't automatically grow up as you get older. Not if you're living right.

So of course, by the time we arrived in Cape May we were already changed into bathing suits and ready to go. It might have been the tail end of September but the water was still warm, and we caught the waves for an hour before we took a late lunch.

That would be enough for one day, right? Just ease into cocktails after lunch, relax on the beach and wait for dinner time. It would have been nice, but instead we parted ways for the time being, and I rode up the back roads of South Jersey to visit my kids at my ex-wife's house. Most people picture New Jersey as this place that overall looks like the land surrounding the Newark Liberty Airport, but it's not true. A huge protected tract of pine lands exists in the middle of the southern half of the state, and when you're riding through there you feel like you're just as far away from civilization as you can get. It's the only nice part of New Jersey, really, other than the beach.

So I took the back way out of Wildwood, through towns like Woodbine, Estell Manor, Dorothy and Buena, up to Medford and met my kids and ex-wife for dinner. They too were glad to have me back in one piece—but I guess I'd feel bad if they weren't!

Each stop was turning into another welcome home celebration, but I wasn't done yet. I dropped in on another friend of mine, Ken and his girlfriend Kate, and had a drink and visited a while. Of course by this time it was getting towards dark and my old friend fatigue was setting in. I had plenty of offers of a place to stay, but I rode another 45 minutes up the road to my sister's house, and crashed there while getting mentally ready for the last day in the saddle.

9/18/10 Saturday

For what I thought were obvious reasons, I didn't want to jump right on the New Jersey Turnpike and ride home on the slab. Instead I came up with a vision of all the cool places I knew on the Delaware river, the western side of the state, and to ride through there on the way home. It was a great scenic, historic journey I'd be going on, but it was way too ambitious. I had already decided that I was going to get home on this day, but the route I had in my head would have been a great two-day ride. I didn't have that figured out when I started.

I got out fairly early, and rode up through Trenton, New Jersey's proud capital, and then crossed the Delaware River where Washington did in the winter of 1776. Of course, I had a bridge to ride over. George had to row. On the Pennsylvania side I went north on Route 32, which is a wonderful, scenic road. History here goes back to the 1700s and earlier, of course, and Route 32 is dotted with 18th century houses and historic inns, little touristy towns like New Hope, and views of the river around every turn. It's a great road, and I'd never ridden it on a motorcycle before, so it was a satisfying adventure.

But it was taking a long time. There wasn't much in the way of traffic, but the road winds all over creation, and it's slow going.

Eventually I got back into New Jersey, to head up through a corner of New York state and into Connecticut, but Jersey is where the traffic started. It was late morning, and every fan of fall splendor was out in force, and there are a lot of people living in rural New Jersey any more. The traffic was stop and go in every little town, at every traffic light, and people were driving like they were the only cars on the road. Someone stopped short in front of me and I locked it up and squared off my tires somewhat, but no mishaps.

It was getting annoying. I worked my way up through the north-western corner of the state, and then slipped over into New York, into even heavier local traffic. People going into garden centers and buying mums, shocks of corn stalks, things for Halloween decoration. Wave an ear of Indian corn in their faces and they all go insane. I finally worked my way up to Route 17, followed it to Route 84, and wisely decided to slab it through Connecticut.

But of course even that wasn't a great idea. Route 84 slowed down in all the usual spots. The only positive thing I could think of is that for the hundreds of times I'd driven on this road, at least I was getting to see it from a bike for the first time. I couldn't help daydreaming back to the high, lonesome roads in North Dakota, Wyoming and Montana; the rolling golden fields of eastern Washington, and the room—the very space between me and everything else out there. The giant blue sky. Even the air molecules felt closer together, back home in the Northeast. Lord knows, I'm not going to knock it, because there's plenty to love in New England, but if we don't learn how to control our reproduction rate in this country, there isn't going to be any place left to stand in 20 more years, let alone sit down.

I had designs of taking Route 84 all the way to Route 91, but by the time I got to Waterbury I couldn't stand the traffic jams any more, and got off onto Route 8 north, my favorite limited access highway. At the northern end, it doesn't take you anywhere more exciting than Winsted, so it suffers much less traffic than most other roads in these parts. Up at the top of Route 8, I know the back way into West Granville, Mass., since I used to live there, so I took

Lynda and Scott King, with the house all ready. Richmond, NH, 9/19/10.

my "secret" back road (part of it isn't paved) and connected with Route 57 and rolled east down towards Granville and Southwick. In Granville you can take a back road into Westfield, and then from Westfield easily get onto the Massachusetts Turnpike and east to Route 91 again, but why bother? Why not go a little farther north and skip Springfield altogether, coming into 91 west of Holyoke. At this point, you are out of the main travel corridors, and all you have to deal with are the few people who think they have found a reason to go up into Vermont. And before ski season, there's not a lot of them. Thankfully.

Does it all sound like a lot of trouble? Yes, it is. The good part about living in New Hampshire is being above all that mess. When you go out for a ride up here, you get roads with little traffic, and the people who are driving aren't driving like they've decided it's okay if they have to kill someone on the way to the mall. I still couldn't shake my daydreams of the Northwest, just a few weeks ago, or the broad expanse of Nevada desert unwinding in front of the bike on the Extraterrestrial Highway. I wasn't even done the trip and I was already homesick for the places I didn't live.

Off of 91 at Route 10, and through the pretty village of Northfield, Mass., before crossing the line into New Hampshire. It was a thrill to see places that are so familiar; places I hadn't seen all summer. Nothing much really changed, but that's okay. Down the hill into Winchester, then up the next hill and into Richmond. I couldn't help but feel my chest tighten up as the last mile rolled by. Finally there's the house, looking like it hadn't been lived in for a while, but my friends Scott and Lynda from Connecticut were there, waiting for me with some food in the refrigerator and all the windows open. It all looked good. It looked like home.

Postcard view of Mt. Ranier, Washington.

Epilogue (07/2011)

Towards the end of the trip, it seemed, as I racked up more miles, I had more and more people ask the question, "Would you do it again?" in some way or another. By that time, well over 10,000 miles into the trip, I would laugh out loud and say, "No effin' way. My memory is too good to want to do this again!"

But you know....

It must be like a recurring disease. Yeah, I put the bike in the back of the garage and didn't look at it for a month after I got home. But then I took it out and washed it, started it up. Dried it off and put it away, but then a few days later I found myself putting on the Gore-Tex and rolling the bike out of the garage. I got on it, on a perfect early fall day, and rolled off a quick 200 mile ride before dinner. I had been thinking that I'd sell the bike and go on to something else, but after that ride I thought maybe I'd just keep that little Suzuki around.

I don't want you to think I'm all starry-eyed, though. Yes, I rode it all summer. But it never became "a part of me..." like you read in a lot of the other long tour 'round-the-world books—like, "The bike and I became one; I felt as if the bike knew exactly where I wanted to go, and it was ready to take me there with only my minimal input." (said in a very dreamy tone of voice). No. That V-Strom fit me perfectly from the start because I worked on it for two weeks to get the handlebars in the exact right spot. Other than that, it was just another infernal machine, ready to break or kill me if I didn't pay attention. When I looked at that camper van in South Dakota, I was serious about being ready to swap vehicles at a moment's notice. If the bike had become a pain in the ass it would have been gone, quickly. This trip, in other words, was all about the trip. It wasn't about the bike.

I passed people along the road, and a surprising number of them, on bicycles all loaded down as heavy as I was. They all looked miserable, on the edge of death. I couldn't understand what sort of internal sins someone must need to atone for in order to put oneself to such torment. So no, I wouldn't be wanting to do it on a bicycle, thank you. I passed walkers; equally as starved-skinny as the bicycle faithful, with huge packs on their backs, laboring east or west under heavy loads, more pilgrims punishing themselves for reasons unknown. If I was going to walk that trip, be assured I would do it with nothing on my back; and with my hands in my pockets at a pace somewhere between a shuffle and a stroll, a pace that drives my fireass girlfriend "Lucille" crazy.

And no, her name isn't Lucy. I picked that name because it has a funny sound.

I guess the point is, we have to find a level of comfort that is acceptable, and still be able to expose as much of our bodies as possible to the open road. If you've been on motorcycles a long time, you know that rain isn't as big of a deal as most people might think it is. You wrap up in the Gore-Tex and keep going. Don't get too close to cars, and don't let the car behind get too close to you. Cold is manageable with electric clothes, and heat is uncomfortable, but as long as you keep hydrating you'll live.

Yep, you get on a nice, quiet bike like the V-Strom, make it fit and wear the right clothes, and crossing the country on a motorcycle isn't too bad of a deal. I guess I could do it again.

Especially now that a year's gone by, and my memory drains away with my advancing age.

There is, after all, that unresolved circumnavigation of Nevada I need to tend to. And I never did get to explore the Badlands of Arizona and New Mexico, places I'd seen out the window of flights from San Diego; places that look dangerously desolate and remote, that just need to be explored closely. Just to see it. And there's always pie waiting, in Pie Town.

Which reminds me, I did send Kathy and Stan Lucy's recipe for caramel-apple upside-down pie, and I'd love to see if they figured out how to bake it.

So yeah, you might see me out there.

Epilogue #2 (01/2017)

I did get out and try to patch up some of the holes in this trip, in the fall of 2013. My friend Dorian, in Olympia, Washington, who had been trying to get me to trade in my Suzuki on a BMW when I stayed with him, was the instigator. In truth, he never really stopped trying to sell me on a GS, and in the summer of 2013 he told me about a friend of his who had a beautiful BMW GS1150 for sale. He sent me the specs on it, and it was outfitted perfectly, just exactly what you'd need for a long ride. The price was right also, and besides that—it was red. What more encouragement did I need?

I made a plan, shipped my riding and navigational gear out to Dorian's house, and in mid-September I flew out to the West Coast for another adventure. I took a couple days touring Seattle with an old friend from the Vancouver/Portland area, and we went to see my new bike—which was actually 15 years old, but looked like brand new.

It was a nice ride. Dorian and I only had a day to try to set it up for me, and we got it together, pretty much. He joined me for the first morning of the ride, and hustled home just before the rain started. I took the long way south through the southern Cascades and through Bend and Burns, Oregon, and into Nevada for a long, lazy loop of that fine state.

I won't go into details on that trip here, but I can refer you to a web site. I did daily postings on GonzoRider.com during that trip, and there are seven separate blog posts about it on GonzoRider; the last time I looked they were still there. If you're interested, check them out—just find the a post called *Taking the Long Way Home* and scroll down to the first post, on September 22. Read up from there, and you might find it amusing.

That trip was supposed to be a quickie, but it only lasted seven days before the BMW gave up a rear drive seal. The delay involved in scheming out a repair strategy allowed some nasty, cold weather to catch up to me, and resulted in a decision to put the bike in storage in Denver, fix it over the winter, and then have a ready bike already out west so I could go ride in the spring. That sounded better than having a storm riding me all the way home, after trusting someone else to fix the bike, and I was happy with my desert tour for the time being. So I had pieces of the BMW shipped home, where I carefully rebuilt the rear drive and shipped all the parts back. The shop where the bike was stored installed everything and had the bike all ready for me when the snow melted in 2014.

And then things got complicated by work and life obligations, and I never managed to get out there for another ride. I sold the bike at a bargain price in late summer of 2014, and haven't been out west on two wheels since.

But I'm not done, not that I'll admit. I've never been attached to a particular bike, so getting geared up for a new riding opportunity is just a matter of thinking of a bike I'd like to try and a place I want to try it, finding one to buy and riding it there. I met a guy just this past summer who, oddly, had a blue "Wee Strom" just like mine, and says he'd like to ride to Alaska one of these days before he gets too old. I never wanted to ride to Alaska, but what the hell. I can think of weirder places I've wound up in my life.

So yeah, once again, you might see me out there.

Statistics

Total Mileage: 14,390 miles

Number of States: 37

Total Time: 67 days

Days Riding: 49

Front tires: 2

Rear tires: 3

Chains: 3

Masterlinks: 5*

Oil changes: 3

*I approached the V-Strom with the same mentality as a dirt biker, and didn't know any better than to use spring-clip o-ring master links on the drive chain. Since this trip a few of my friends have patiently tried to explain that on a road-going bike a standard masterlink is a very bad idea, and that the only way to link a road bike chain is to rivet it on with a special tool. Who knew? All of my chain problems were caused by a typical spring-clip masterlink that shouldn't have been there. I'm sure I still would have worn out two chains on the trip, but I wouldn't have had a nagging problem with masterlink wear if, duh, I didn't use a standard master link.

Other titles by Paul Clipper

available at www.amazon.com,
paperbacks available from CreateSpace.com/catalog#

The Art of Trailriding (Kindle) #B005OJZW32; (Paper) 6736202
33 How-to-Ride columns written over a three year period in *Trail Rider* magazine, offering instruction on how to improve your riding skills and increase your off-road fun. Each chapter covers a specific aspect of riding or bike setup, and presents easy solutions to solving the problems you might experience on the trail. Amazon reviews: "I'm 45 years young and brand new to dirt bikes. I've had my bike about 3 months and logged about 400km's in a variety of terrain. I've fallen off plenty of times with no injuries and despite riding with groups of experienced riders and watching "how-to" DVD's, I was still missing the basics. This book was excellent in educating me on the basics of bike setup, balance and control techniques."

ISDE 1982: Povaska Bystrica, Czechoslovakia: (Paper) 6834033
In 1982, the USA sent 25 motorcyclists to the other side of the Iron Curtain to compete in the International Six Day Enduro. The premier team from this group of riders, the USA Word Trophy Team, rode like champions that week, and finished the penultimate day as the overall winners of the event. This is the story of that week as I saw it go down. A 14,000 word reminiscence of the trip there and the race, along with 105 photos from the event.

Nevada Rally: The American Adventure *(Kindle)* # B009JWHKQW
There are motorcycle events every weekend, but truly epic events only happen on the rare occasion. The Nevada Rally was such an event. Planned and executed by Franco Acerbis and his Acerbis Adventure team, the Nevada Rally swept into the Silver State in 1993 and created a sensation that is still talked about today. A compilation of all three years of the rally, illustrated.

The Best of Last Over, Volume 2 (Kindle) # B005SS6QX4
A collection of Last Over magazine columns from *Trail Rider Magazine*, from 1987 through 1989. Funny stories, informative stories and foolishness about dirt bikes and dirt bike riders, taken from the beginning years of Paul Clipper's tenure at *Trail Rider*. From Amazon reviews: "If you ride or would like to ride street, dirt etc...this is a great read and timeless. Really if you ride this is worth the price of admission."

The Best of Last Over, Volume 3 (Kindle) # B006HC9K9W
A collection of Last Over magazine columns from *Trail Rider Magazine*, from 1990 through 1992. As if one reprise of Best of Last Over wasn't enough, here's another one to round out the collection. More humorous stories about dirt bikers and dirt bikes that are easy reading and fun. I love quoting Amazon reviews: "Paul Clipper's "Last Over" collection has soul, pretension? Nope, just the straight dope." What does it mean? Who knows—it sounds good! An inexpensive book that will help fill your Kindle with dirt biking screed, and give you something to read in the dead of winter.

(Check Amazon often to see what's new. More books by Paul Clipper are in the works, and some of the Kindle books will be transfered to CreateSpace paperbacks soon.)